A Servant Of Christ

by

Reverend Randy C. Brodhagen

(A Guide to Holy Spirit Ministry)

A SERVANT OF CHRIST

By Reverend Randy C. Brodhagen

(A Guide to Holy Spirit Ministry)

Glory to God Ministries, International,
67-399 Palm Canyon Drive, Cathedral City, CA,
Mailing Address P.O. Box 4167, Palm Springs, CA 92263, (760) 321-5222.

ISBN: 978-0-692-29738-4

Published by
GLORY TO GOD MINISTRIES INTERNATIONAL
P.O. Box 4167
Palm Springs, CA 92263
www.glorytogod.org

Printed in the United States of America.

TABLE OF CONTENTS

ACKNOWLEDGEMENTS

This book is dedicated to the glory of God. May the Lord richly bless my parents Floyd and Bette, wife Diana, children Erin and Jesse, and all who are in my heart who have played a role in the Lord's divine destiny and plan for my life.

INTRODUCTION

To everything born under heaven there is a time, a season, a purpose, a plan, and a destiny. The Lord knows our beginning from our end. He has called us to be to the praise of His glory and to fulfill the purpose to which He has called each of us.

We are not on this earth merely to occupy time and space, be born, grow up, make friends, get married — have children, make money, experience life's good times and hardships, make memories, and die. The Lord has much more for us. The Lord says, *"For I know the plans I have for you, plans to prosper you and not to harm you, plans to give you hope and a future."* (Jeremiah 29:11-12) Jesus says, *"The thief comes only to steal and kill and destroy; but I have come that they may have life, and have it to the full."* (John 10:10)

The self-made man fashions a life around himself. The visions, plans, dreams, provision, relationships, money, loves and desires are centered around what people want to see happen for their lives and who and what pertains to them. Empires rise and fall, but only what is of the Lord will remain.

The God-made man allows the Lord to fashion His image, visions, plans, dreams, provision, relationships, money, loves and desires. The God-made man has his steps of life ordered of the Lord to accomplish God's eternal purpose. He is eternal and his works remain because God is eternal, and He is doing the work in and through His God-made man. (Philippians 1:6, 2:12-13) The God-made man builds the kingdom of God.

As the Holy Spirit has directed, this book is written to glorify God with the intention to draw you into His loving presence and to help you to realize, experience, and fulfill the call and destiny of God in your life. THIS BOOK IS A GUIDE TO HOLY SPIRIT MINISTRY.

Know that you are God's good workmanship, created by God to honor and glorify the Lord (Ephesians 2:10) and to work the works of God which the Lord has given you to do in this life. (John 14:12-14) Before you enjoy His presence eternally in the new heaven and new earth, you have people to see and things to do for the kingdom of heaven. Enjoy your life now as you allow the good Lord to shape and develop you into His image and fulfill God's plan for your life.

A Servant Of

CHRIST

PART 1

BEGINNINGS

Chapter One

THE SELF-MAN vs. THE GOD-MAN

Only the Lord has no beginning and no end. We are all created by God for God. Unfortunately people don't realize that fact because we live in a natural world and people look to natural sources and explanations rather than to divine knowledge and wisdom.

The Lord said to Jeremiah, *"Before I formed you in the womb I knew (called) you, before you were born I set you apart;"* (Jeremiah 1:5) For God chose us in Christ Jesus before the creation of the world to be holy and blameless in His sight. (See Ephesians 1:3-14)

The people did not recognize Jesus' divine descent: "Isn't this Joseph's son?" (Luke 3:23, 4:22, 8:20-21, 1:34-37) Jesus is God come in the flesh. (1st John 4:2) *"But as many as received Him* [Jesus as Lord, born again], *to them He gave the right to become children of God, to those who believe in His name: who were born, not of blood, nor of the will of the flesh, nor the will of man, but of God."* (John 1:12-13 KJV)

We who believe in Jesus as Lord and Savior have become children of God — born not of natural descent, nor of human decision or a husband's or wife's will, but born of God. We were in the heart of God before the world began and now through faith in Jesus have entered into the family of God to carry out His purpose in the earth.

The self-man believes human bloodline is important — money, fame, relationship, power, health, race, etc., determine his destiny. The God-man knows that God determines our destiny and directs our steps as

He wills, to His glory. We are of God's bloodline through faith in Jesus. As we live, obeying God's wisdom, the Lord gives to each of us what we need to fulfill His plan for our lives. (Read Proverbs 3 and 4)

The Lord uses all the things that the self-man trusts in — relationships, money, power, health, etc.; however, it is the Lord's presence and blessing in one's life that makes the difference. Without the Lord we can do nothing to accomplish His purpose in our lives, even if we had all of the other things that the self-man thinks are necessary to be successful in life. (Philippians 3)

"Godliness with contentment is great gain. For we brought nothing into the world and we can take nothing out..." (1st Timothy 6:6-7 thru 16) *"Trust in the Lord with all your heart and lean not to your own understanding; in all your ways acknowledge Him and He will direct your paths."* (Proverbs 3:5-6) *"Let your conduct be without covetousness; be content with such things as you have. For He Himself has said, 'I will never leave you nor forsake you.' So we may boldly say: 'The Lord is my helper; I will not fear. What can man do to me?' "* (Hebrews 13:5-6 KJV) *"I have loved you with an everlasting love; I have drawn you with loving-kindness."* (Jeremiah 31:3) *"Call to me and I will answer you and tell you great and unsearchable things you do not know."* (Jeremiah 33:3) *"Be Holy because I, the Lord your God is holy."* (Leviticus 19:2)

TRAIN UP A CHILD...

From my youth I had the privilege of being taught the word of God like these scriptures. I learned about God's ways for good and the devil's ways for evil. Train up a child in the way of the Lord and when he gets older he will not depart from it. I was raised to honor God and His authorities, to obey the Ten commandments, to love, seek, and believe God, to love people, to do to others what I want done for me, to know the Lord loves me, is with me, has a good plan for my life, and nothing is too hard for the Lord to do.

I know that at whatever time in a person's life he comes under the Lordship of Jesus Christ, he will be blessed by doing these principles which will cause him to grow in favor with God and man. (Proverbs 3:1-6, Luke 2:39-40)

The words of 1st and 2nd Timothy, the book of Proverbs for wisdom of living, and Ecclesiastes for perspective on priorities of life have always been important to me in learning God's ways. From a child I always wanted to serve the Lord. I did not know what I was going to do or how to do it, but I wanted to serve the Lord with all my heart.

My parents sought to love my two sisters, my brother and me. They taught biblical right from wrong, disciplined us when we needed correction, provided for us, went to church, and gave us a Christian parochial school education. I am thankful to God for my parents, Floyd and Bette, my sisters, Alice and Shirley, and my brother, David.

Years later, my wife, Diana and I provided the same environment for our children Erin and Jesse. We realized what children learn and are exposed to in early years has a great effect on their lives. As Joshua said, *"As for me and my house, we will serve the Lord."*

Even children are known by their ways. What we choose and do with our environment will make the difference in how it all turns out. If we seek the Lord and do good, we will be blessed. If we seek our own ways and do not do what God says, we curse ourselves. "I am Jesus' little lamb, ever glad at heart I am."

Nobody owes you anything. Life does not owe you anything. If you want anything, you need to work and do your best at it. I mowed grass and had a morning and evening paper route by the age of ten.

I learned this: be thankful for what you have; and if you do not like what you have, do something to change it. Take nothing or no one for granted — appreciate God, people, and what you have. Do not look for someone to give you something. You give and then you receive. Be responsible for your life and actions.

Do whatever you do with all your heart in the name of Jesus to the glory of God. (1st Corinthians 10:31, Colossians 3:17) Many times children get into trouble because they do not have discipline and structure in their lives. Rules are good and not made to be broken, but to be kept, because they lead to blessing when they are obeyed. Rebellion is of the devil. Honor authority.

Live life by God's principles, not by your desires, and you will succeed. *"Delight yourself in the Lord and He will give you the desires of your heart."* (Psalm 37:3-4)

The Lord taught me discipline and principles through His Word (John 15:3), rules at home, church, school, athletics, and work. I learned to be responsible, to obey, and complete those disciplines if I was to excel. Diligent hands prosper. Laziness leads to poverty. A tender heart and conscience is a good, God thing. No short cuts. Practice-practice-practice, and play by the rules. Boredom is a state of mind — if you do not put anything in you will get nothing out. You decide what you will have. Believe God and do not give up. (Joshua 1:5-9)

I thank the Lord for parents, teachers, pastors, coaches, and employers who cared about me enough to use what God has given them to do to teach, encourage, motivate, inspire, rebuke and correct me, to develop and bring out God's best in me. I now have that same desire to bring out the Lord's best in you.

The Lord is concerned about results. Therefore, I am concerned about results. If we follow the Lord's principles, rules, and directions we will be blessed. (Proverbs 3:5-6) The results in my younger years were: I did not bring shame or disgrace to the Lord, my parents, brother or sisters — no alcohol, or addictions — honor roll student — four year letterman (baseball) — blessed at work — youth leader at church. A God ordered and blessed childhood.

GOD HAS MADE A PLAN FROM START TO FINISH

Since the Lord has a purpose and plan for each of our lives, the thief wants to mess up God's plan through the use of temptations, trials, and attacks — spiritually, mentally, physically, financially, and in relationships. (1st Peter 5:8-9) Such attacks come at different times in our lives to attempt to get us to give up on our faith in God, ruin God's plan for our lives, and hinder God from receiving glory and us being with Him.

However, what the devil intended for evil, the Lord will turn to good and God's glory as we put our faith and trust in Him. Consider the life of Joseph, Moses, Jesus, Paul, etc. Joseph's brothers tried to kill him and sold him into slavery. Pharaoh tried to kill Moses, but the Lord put him in Pharaoh's courts. The thief tried to take all of their lives, but God intervened.

Put your faith in God that you are not going to leave this world until you have finished everything that the good Lord wants you to do!

When you are about to be or are about God's business, temptations, distractions, afflictions, and persecutions will come (Psalm 34, 2nd Corinthians 3), but remember *"Many are the afflictions of the righteous, but the Lord delivers him out of them all."* (Psalm 34:19) The Lord wants us to begin and finish what He has given to each of us. Flee youthful (and not so youthful) lusts. (2nd Timothy 2:22)

In my youth physical sickness and disease were sent by the devil to harm me. While the Lord was developing His character, desire, purpose, and plan in me, the thief was trying to kill me.

I learned what it was like to be on both sides of the hospital bed. I had not learned about healing, and no one had taught me about healing. The Lord says, *"My people are destroyed for lack of knowledge."* (Hosea 4:6)

After I was born something attacked my body which the doctors thought was polio. I would not get a sore throat except it became strep throat. A cut would become blood poisoning. Colon conditions and migraine headaches would come. Pain inflicted my body, but the tests would show me to be the "perfect specimen of health." (I did not know then about spirits of infirmity.) No one knew what to do or what was going on!

When I was sixteen, something happened that set direction for my life and the ministry that the Lord had called me to do. My family purchased a spider monkey. It had not had all of its shots and was a carrier of disease, and I was the one who took care of it. The monkey died. Most of the family was in the hospital, and I was bed ridden for over four months, nearly dying at several points. My liver shut down. My tongue was swollen and I could not eat. I was jaundiced with excretion and itching sores on my body. I had no strength to stand or walk. After months had passed, when I was able to think clearly again, I completed two semesters of school work in one semester.

Being the perfectionist I was, I received honor roll grades, only to discover that I then had a stomach ulcer. For several months I heard a thought telling me, *You're going to have a stomach ulcer.* I did not know then whether it was God telling me what was going to happen to prepare me, or the thief speaking thoughts into my head trying to make me believe a harmful thing, so it happened. (Job 3:25)

In any case, the ulcer happened and now I had to deal with it — milk, toast, cream, etc. I sought the Lord to help me. One day as I was reading my Bible, Philippians 4:4-19 came to my attention.

"Rejoice in the Lord always. I will say it again: Rejoice! Let your gentleness be evident to all. The Lord is near. Do not be anxious about anything, but in everything, by prayer and petition, with thanksgiving, present your requests to God. And the peace of God, which transcends all understanding, will guard your hearts and your minds in Christ Jesus. Finally, brother, whatever is true, whatever is noble, whatever is right, whatever is pure, whatever is lovely, whatever is admirable — if anything is excellent or praiseworthy — think about such things. Whatever you have learned or received or heard from me, or seen in me — put it into practice. And the God of peace will be with you." (Philippians 4:4-9)

"I know what it is to be in need, and I know what it is to have plenty. I have learned the secret of being content in any and every situation, whether well fed or hungry, whether living in plenty or in want. I can do everything through him who gives me strength." (Philippians 4:12-13)

"And my God will meet all your needs according to his glorious riches in Christ Jesus." (Philippians 4:19)

It was as if the Lord was talking to my situation and to my life. I read it aloud over and over. Then I started to do what it said. The peace of God came upon me, and my stomach stopped hurting. The pain disappeared and the tests showed the ulcer was gone. I was healed. My liver also showed no evidence of any damage from the disease the monkey had died from. (At 62 years, the doctor informed me at my physical that I had the liver of a 25 year old. Praise God!)

I was learning that the Lord is my healer. The Lord had turned what was intended for evil into a praise report to His glory. He then proceeded to teach me about righteousness (right standing), peace, and joy in the Lord.

Perfectionism is not of God because it is me seeking to live life and accomplish things in my own strength and ability, rather than allowing God to work in me and through me. In Christ Jesus I am perfect. I am lacking nothing. (2nd Peter 1:3-5) I am full of joy and peace because God is in control. I am fulfilled by God's presence. (Psalm 23) I am content because I know who I have believed and I am fully persuaded and convinced that He is able to keep that in which I have committed to Him. (2nd Timothy 1:12; Philippians 4:12)

I had thought I was allowing God to lead me. I had thought what I was doing was to His glory, but apparently worry, stress, and striving are not of peace and not of God. They are symptoms of self-effort, rather than relying on God's strength and ability. The result in the physical was ulcers, colitis, headaches, high blood pressure, etc. The result in the mental realm is no peace and joy and no ability to enjoy life.

I was doing what many Christians think is godly — "God helps those who help themselves." Help themselves to what? What a deception! Apart from Christ Jesus I can do nothing. (John 15:5) I asked God's forgiveness for my pride and He healed me and gave me right standing, peace, and joy in the Lord. I was learning that the Lord is my perfection, peace, and joy.

PROMOTION COMES FROM THE LORD

Once feeling healthy again, I felt like I needed to get different employment while attending high school. As you delight in the Lord, the Lord gives you the desires which He has put in your heart. As you trust Him with your life, not leaning to your own understanding, acknowledging Him in all your ways, then the Lord will direct your steps. (Proverbs 3:5-6)

I asked the Lord to lead me in the job hunting process as I put out my applications. The impression was given to me to accept the first job opening that came to me. I was hired by a major department store to work in the lawn and garden department which also became the toy department during Christmas. Starting pay was $1.35 per hour.

A week later I received two other job opportunities which paid three and five times more. However, I thanked them, declining the offers because I had made a commitment to my new employer.

Integrity, commitment and faithfulness to God, yourself, and others is more important for one's life than chasing "a better offer." Advancement and promotion comes from the Lord. (1st Peter 5:6) I was obedient to follow what I believed the Lord had put in my heart about the first offer. Sure enough, in six months the garden and toy department went on commission sales. Now, as a 17 year old working 16 hours a week, I was earning as much as the main appliance salesman upstairs.

The Lord knows the future for His plans for our lives. We need to trust and obey Him. If I had settled for the higher paying jobs and not done what the Lord directed, I would have missed the blessing. Furthermore, this job with good grade scholarships enabled me to pay for all my college education. When I transferred to college back east, the store was three blocks from the campus.

I was learning that the Lord is my provider. *"My God shall supply all your needs according to His riches in glory in Christ Jesus."* (Philippians 4:19) I honored God with my giving and He honored me.

God's favor will create jealousy (remember the lives of Jacob and Joseph) at various points in your life. Do not get bitter. Just love people and do what the Lord has given you to do. I remember that after college was completed I was promised a 40 hour work week; however, that never happened. A longtime person in the department persuaded the manager to keep cutting my hours. I did not complain, although the thought crossed my mind. I submitted my cause to the Father who judges justly. (1st Peter 2:13-23) The Lord caused people to come and purchase on my shift. I made more than I was making with less hours.

Finally, when I was decreased to 10 hours a week, still earning as much as before, the Lord directed me to take the last month of summer off and see my family — a vacation before I started seminary in the Fall. I had made enough for school and for a vacation. God is good! Just like Jacob, God blessed me. (See Genesis)

During college the Lord was preparing me for His purpose. Majoring in social psychology and philosophy, I learned from the Lord how people think and why they do what they do for better or worse. I was learning to search the motivation of my own heart — why I thought what I thought and did what I did.

RECEIVING INSTRUCTIONS AND CORRECTION

In the on-going saga of life and adventure in the Holy Spirit we are always given opportunities to learn and to grow closer to God and to know our own heart. The Lord is making us into His image (Romans 8:29), and He wants to teach us His ways. We need to be open to learn, listen, and to obey. Foolishness is bound up in the heart of a child, but the rod of correction drives it away. Unfortunately, we can grow up and still be playing the fool by not receiving correction and instruction. A wise man loves and desires it because it makes him wiser and more excellent (to God's glory).

I remember three incidents of correction in my early years which impacted my life (and a fourth which presented a challenge). When I was eight years old, my family and I were all in church. Mom was in the choir while dad was taking care of us in the roped-off children's section. I was minding my own business and had hooked the aisle chord on my dad's new suit pocket. The rest is history. My sister let out a scream. My dad grabbed her, racing out of the row. The sound of the ripping of the suit could be heard over the pastor's voice. I knew I was going to get disciplined... and did. My dad disciplined me for tearing the suit, and the Lord disciplined me for not paying attention to God's Word in His house.

The second correction occurred in my third year of college. Our speech instructor had assessed the student body five dollars each for an unexplained reason. That day it was my turn to do a five-minute persuasion speech. In five minutes the entire class was incited to find out what the bill was about. The explanation was in our mail boxes that afternoon.

My teacher called me in for evaluation of the speech. I thought I had done rather well in that everyone was persuaded, including the teacher. However, the teacher gave me a different grade than I had anticipated.

The Lord speaks through the authorities in our lives. My teacher told me, "Randy, the Lord has given you a gift to move the multitudes when you speak. Be sure to move them in the way the Lord wants them to go!"

"A man's ways appear right to a man, but the Lord searches the motivation of the heart." (Proverbs 16:2) We need to know our own heart.

The third correction occurred in seminary. Being foolish, I asked the teacher a question, but I already knew the answer. The teacher responded, "I will not answer that question because it is just intended to create problems." I knew he was correct.

Foolishness is not a part of a wise man's life. I knew better, but was trying to draw attention to me, rather than to the Lord. I asked the teacher's and the class' forgiveness. A godly man cannot be involved in foolishness or his own purpose.

The challenge came to me in the first grade when my teacher said to the class, "I will be towards you the way you make me to be." I knew if I was an obedient and studious boy, I would learn and grow in God and be blessed.

The Lord says, *"God opposes the proud but shows favor to the humble."* (James 4:6)

When I graduated from seminary, my first grade teacher wrote me a note of encouragement. She told me how she had watched and prayed for me over the years, and was thanking the Lord for the godly man I had become. I will never forget the love and care of the Lord through this woman of God.

The Lord places people in our lives to speak into our lives and help us to become who He intends us to be. I thank the Lord for every one of those people — past, present, and future. God bless you all!

DISCIPLINE AND PRIORITIES

Studying to show myself a workman approved to the Lord, I grew in God's Word. Books that the Lord used to influence my life during the college years were The Cost of Discipleship by Dietrich Bonhoeffer and The God Players by Earl Jabay.

Aware that temptations and distractions are constantly trying to steal and destroy God's purpose for our lives, especially in those years, I devoted myself to my studies leading campus activities, sports, caring for people at church, and working a job.

My time was fully occupied and focused — focused on God, right things. Discretion and discipline will keep us out of trouble. When loneliness came, I had no time to be lonely. I had girl friends but could not get caught up in the personal relationships which would hinder me from reaching the goal set before me. (I had purposed early in my life not to marry until I had finished my education. I brought my wife with me to celebrate my last year of seminary.)

About the time you think you stand, take heed lest you fall. (1st Corinthians 10:12) Pride of life (1st John 2:6-7 NKJ) is a subtle temptation. Everything I set my hand to do prospered as the Lord says will happen. (Joshua 1:5-9) I had favor with God and man (Proverbs 3:4), seeking to do whatever I did with all my heart in the name of Jesus to the glory of God. (Colossians 3:23)

One late evening in my second year of seminary, I came home to my dorm room. Opening the door, I was immediately engulfed in an extremely thick fog. Falling to my knees, I began to weep. The Lord's presence had filled the room with His glory. All things are exposed in God's presence or by His Word. (Hebrews 4:12)

"Son, I cannot use you the way you are," the Lord said to me. Sobbing uncontrollably, I asked the Lord, "What have I done?" (All my life I had wanted to serve the Lord.)

The Lord proceeded to show me my life on a movie screen. One-two-three-four — He itemized by priority, the things of my life that I was doing for Him. He was number six on the list of twelve things.

My relationship with the Lord as my first love had five other loves before Him. The Lord said, "Son, if you love what you are doing more than the One you are doing it for, it profits nothing!"

The Lord did not say I was not saved. He said He could not use me for the purpose He had called me to unless I humbled myself and returned to my first love, namely Himself. (Revelations 2) Immediately I asked and received the Lord's forgiveness. (1st John 1:9) I began thanking and praising the Lord for His love to me that I should be His child. (1st John 3:1-3) He loves and cares about me enough to discipline and correct me, giving me an opportunity to change and fulfill what He called and destined me to do. (Ephesians 2:10)

The priority list on the screen changed. I saw the Lord go to the number one position, and everything else ordered out. If we put the

Lord first in all our ways, He will direct the path and priorities. (Psalm 37, Proverbs 3:5-6)

The Lord began to instruct me. In my younger years, I could not figure out why faith was not the greatest of the three: faith, hope, and love. (1st Corinthians 13:13) I believed God's Word and promises and acted on them. Then God blessed me. *"Without faith it is impossible to please God, because anyone who comes to Him must believe that He exists, and that he is a rewarder of those who earnestly seek Him."* (Hebrews 11:6)

What the Lord showed me was that it is not about my faith, hope, or love, nor my seeking Him. Rather it is all about the Lord in His love sought me out first and gave Himself (Jesus) for me and for everyone that we might be saved and have God's faith, hope, and love. He did this for His name's sake and glory, not mine. Salvation and abundant life are all about the Lord and who He is — love, not my predicament, ability or lack of it! I understood.

As morning drew near, I drove to the church that I was working with and delivered that "Jesus first" message which was fresh from the throne of God. (Since that night in God's presence I have purposed to deliver nothing but "fresh" Word to God's people). (John 6:63)

Following the service an older man came to me, saying, "Pastor, I have been in the church all of my life. But today I asked God's forgiveness for living my life the way I wanted. I received the love of God in Jesus Christ as my first love. Thank you for sharing God's heart with me." As the Lord had changed me, so He changed him while I shared God's Word of life from heaven.

At different times in your life there will occur divine "revival" or awakenings. From that time on, a "freshness" in the Lord and an increased intensity or urgency arose within me about the Lord's return.

Along with God's other ministries, I was to prepare the way for the Lord's return. People need to be ready with Jesus as their "first love."

WHAT IS MINISTRY?

My internship year of seminary was spent in Wilmington, Delaware. I had just come back from planting a church in Arizona. The Lord's preparation may have you go to different places and people in order to experience what He wants you to know and do (wildernesses experience, Moses, Paul, etc.).

During this time I learned the importance of a minister's character. Ministry is not about position or using one's position for personal gain. It is about caring for God's people.

I was placed in a position where the head minister taught me how to use my position for personal gain. It was a wealthy church. Everyone was wonderful to me, but the Lord was showing me that being a minister of God is not a job or occupation. It is a calling to teach and serve God, caring for His people, not them serving you.

The pastor said to me one day when I was preparing to go back to seminary, "Randy, you really believe this stuff, don't you?"

Not everyone in the ministry is a minister. Paul said, "I have no one else like Timothy who has a genuine care for the people." (Philippians 2:20-21) It does not matter what motivation people preach Christ as long as Christ is preached. (Philippians 1:15-18) Like marriage, people go in the ministry for many of the wrong reasons. They will not last.

It is not for me to judge another, but it is for me to observe and to learn my own heart and motivation. For each man or woman stands accountable to God. (1st Corinthians 4:1-5)

Several years later the pastor left the ministry to become a salesman, which he would do very well. There are many reasons why we do what we do. I had asked him, "How can you do something (be a pastor) that you don't believe in?" You have to do what you are given to do and glorify God in that vocation. His wife's dad was a minister.

I had to know in myself what my heart was to do and what the Lord wanted for me. I loved this man and his family. I wanted to see God's best for them all.

"As iron sharpens iron, so one person sharpens another." (Proverbs 27:17)

I thank the Lord in remembrance of them and the church people for their kindness to me and for all I learned and experienced during that time of training. Ministers are people, like everyone else. We all have our strengths and weaknesses — moments in and out of God. We need the Lord and each other's support, prayers, and encouragement to do what we are given from heaven to do and complete our calling.

When I was just twelve years old, the pastor and his secretary committed adultery. The whole church fell apart. I asked the question, "Why is the church falling apart because the pastor has a problem? Our faith is in God. We need to forgive and pray for him to get help."

GETTING RID OF A POVERTY SPIRIT

It was during my training for ministry in Delaware that I also was being delivered of a poverty spirit. There is a balance to everything in life. I was raised to work hard, be content, be generous to God and others, save your money, be frugal, live modestly, pay your bills, and never beg.

Upon my arrival, the pastor and people wanted me to live in a nice place and have nice things like they had. I chose an inexpensive place so I could save my money. That is what I decided, but was that what the Lord wanted for me?

One day a man came to my office and told me that the Lord wanted him to give me (personally) a check, not for the ministry. I declined, telling him that I was alright and that we had other needs for the ministry. No sooner did he leave my office, the Lord spoke to me, "Son, do you know the joy that you have when you give? You just stole that man's joy and blessing in giving."

The poverty spirit (pride) that I had hindered me from receiving. The Lord was blessing me and I was turning down His blessing which was coming through this man and hindered his blessing in giving to me in obedience to the Lord. Nobody was getting blessed.

The Lord says, *"Give, and it will be given unto you* [you will receive] — *pressed down, shaken together, running over shall people* [under the Lord's direction] *give to you."* (Luke 6:38) You will receive more than you give so you can give more. (2nd Corinthians 9)

The Lord impressed me to run after the man. I caught him as he was about to drive off. Explaining what the Lord had told me, I apologized and asked him if he was still willing to do what the Lord had sent him to do. He was overjoyed and handed me the check which I gladly received, thanking the Lord and him for God's provision through him. I prayed for him that the Lord would bless him exceedingly (which the Lord did!).

You would think that we would learn, but time goes by and we forget. Several years later the Lord had to discipline me again in relation to that poverty spirit. I was pastoring a church in California. I never would talk about money because I did not want people to think that we only want their money. That is all some people talk about because your money is all they want. God is the source of the minister and the people.

There is a balance that the Lord was teaching me. He rebuked me, "You are not teaching My people how to honor Me and prosper, nor are you giving them opportunity to give to Me and My work." (I tithed but I did not teach the people about the tithe or offering at that time. Now I do.)

"You are hindering My people from their prosperity" the Lord said. The only place in the Bible where God says "Put Me to the test" is in relation to the tithe (10% gross income off of the top) and offerings. (Malachi 3:10-12; 2nd Corinthians 9)

I was hindering the people from being blessed by fearing they would think I had a greedy money-grabbing heart. (2nd Corinthians 2:17) In reality, it was God calling for the tithe and offering. All I was to do was to be obedient to Him and teach and allow people to honor Him through their giving (Luke 6:38) and be blessed.

Greedy people will not give to God no matter what motivation you have in calling for the tithe and offering. The Lord will deal with the greedy ministers and other people alike.

As a man and minister of God, I cannot allow my doubts, fears, opinions, traditions, and prejudices to veil or cloud the Word of God's Truth from the people. People share and do what they believe or do not believe. God's Word, not our opinion, sets people free.

Lord, forgive us for our pride, and unbelief, disobedience and ignorance of your Word and ways. What does God's Word say? *Help us to humble ourselves to learn to do things Your way and be willing to courageously change that Your will be done on earth as in heaven in us and through us.* (1st Peter 5:6-9) *Help us to be seekers and doers of your Truth. Reveal your Truth to us, Lord, in Jesus' name.*

A DIVINE APPOINTMENT

One day in Delaware I was in need of some car repair and tire work. I asked my senior pastor where I might find a good tire shop. He referred me to one and told me to be sure to wear my clergy collar so I would get a discount. I am not rebellious, but I could not wear my clergy collar to get a discount. While sitting in the waiting room, a young woman came downstairs from the management offices. I began to speak with her and be friendly.

"He or she who would have friends must show themselves friendly." (Proverbs 18:24)

She asked me about myself. I told her I was new in the area and had come from St. Louis. She asked what had brought me to Delaware. I told her, "I am the assistant pastor at the Lutheran church."

Her response was interesting to me, "Yes, and I'm Lady Godiva" (she had long, flowing, brown hair). (Remember, I did not have on my clergy collar which to many people recognize as a priest or minister, not for discount purposes.) But then again if I had worn the collar she would have known that I was telling the truth. (Maybe I was wrong in judging my authority's motives. Just maybe we had the Holy Spirit using him.)

I laughed. We talked some more before she had to leave. It does not take me long to get to know a person. The Lord reveals things.

Diana is witty, perceptive, playful, down-to-earth, lovely (inside and out), and truthful with a great sense of justice. But it was the sincere, tender gentle (humble) heart open to grow and see the truth of God that caught my attention. Always remember what attracted you to your spouse.

I went looking for friendship while in Delaware, so I asked her if she would be willing to see me again in another setting. She was willing to go to lunch, but not to dinner.

A few weeks later, I took her to lunch to what I was told was a nice place — but when we arrived it was closed for health reasons. Great start! — But bless God it got better!

God wants us to seldom reflect on the days of our lives, for He wants to occupy our time with gladness of heart. (Ecclesiastes 5:19-20) I wanted Diana to seldom reflect on anyone else but me, so I occupied her time for the next months until we were married. I always want her to be glad of heart.

WHAT IS IT ALL ABOUT?

Many times the Lord puts things in your heart before your head. A few weeks into the relationship I told Diana, "I'm not going to marry you, and you are not going to marry me, so let's just have a good time together while I'm here."

She thought that I was a pervert, wanting her body like the others. Her mama told her that I was different. She did not think that was what I meant. Thank God! I did not mean that.

Remember, I had always purposed not to marry until I was finished with my schooling, and I had one year left. The Lord had another plan. She was to compliment me in that last year. I did not want to go into the relationship needy or as a burden to her, but rather as a blessing.

There was something else that surfaced at this time which I did not realize until about 30 years later when I was invited to do a seminar session on "Marriage and the Ministry." At times, there was a subconscious tension or fear within me that my love for Diana would take me away from the Lord being my first love. This is what caused Adam and Solomon to fall away from the Lord. Abraham listened to Sarah and missed God. (Later the Lord told Abraham to listen to Sarah [the compliment working] but you don't hear much about that).

I even verbalized this to Diana before we were married. "You will be the second love of my life," I told her. For a moment, I saw her hurt. Then I responded, "That is not a bad thing being second to the Lord. I don't ever want to put you in a position where you will have to choose between me and the Lord. I know you will choose the Lord. I don't ever want you to put me in a position where I will have to choose between you or the Lord because I will choose the Lord."

The test was to come. The Lord knows our beginning from our end and His plans are for good, not for evil, plans to prosper and give us a future. Diana was not the problem. Eve was not the problem. Solomon's wives were not the problem. The problem or question is "Will the man of God stand up and lovingly lead and care for his wife God's way?

The Lord was preparing for what lay ahead for me and countless others concerning marriage and ministry.

We must live our lives and make our decisions based on God's principles, not on our or others' feelings. We must be flexible to allow God and others to change our plans, trusting that the Lord has His plans and is in control of everything pertaining to our lives. (Jeremiah 29:11-12; 2nd Timothy 1:12, Proverbs 3:5-6)

Life is happening on many levels at once. We truly need to trust the Lord, lean not to our own understanding, acknowledge Him in all our ways and He will direct the path spiritually, mentally, physically, financially, and in our relationships.

While Diana and I were preparing to be married, my dad and mom had gotten a divorce and the Lutheran church body I belonged to had divided, forming a break off seminary. The majority of my friends went there. We were now faced with more decisions about where I was going to return to seminary and what would be our future.

I understand what Jesus was saying, *"Seek first the kingdom of God,"* and God will take care of you. *"Don't worry about tomorrow, for tomorrow will worry about itself. Each day has enough trouble of its own."* (Matthew 6:33-34)

Diana and I purposed a commitment to God and each other in regard to the marriage, "Until natural death do us part." Rebellion and political selfish ambition is not of God, so I purposed to return to the existing seminary. (Do not get caught up in another's controversy or you will lose your focus to seek and build the kingdom of God.) Selfish power and politics have no place in God's church. Beware of selfish ambition — yours or others.

BEGINNING LIFE TOGETHER

The last year of seminary was the first year of our marriage. The Lord had provided full scholarships for tuition and housing removing financial pressure. God's favor and diligence in study, good grades, and faithful commitment (president of student body — previously student activities) provide rewards. Diana worked by her choice to help do her part, not out of necessity. She has always been such a blessing.

The Lord positioned us in the spacious place where our marriage could grow. So many times people put themselves under pressure by not preparing properly for what they are undertaking or they have wrong priorities. Life has enough pressure without us making more on our own.

It was a building and growing together year both for the seminary and for our marriage. A new foundation was being laid. New beginnings are exciting and challenging. We must allow the Lord to direct our path.

Trust, cooperation, and self-sacrifice are essential for growth. Anything that involves people — marriage, friendship, church, business, or government needs the partnership working of trust, cooperation, and self-sacrifice. Paul said, *"If you have any encouragement from being united with Christ, if any comfort from his love, if any fellowship with the Spirit, if any tenderness and compassion, then make my joy complete by being like-minded, having the same love, being one in spirit and purpose. Do nothing out of selfish ambition or vain conceit, but in humility consider others better than yourselves. Each of you should look not only to your own interests, but also to the interests of others. Your attitude should be the same as that of Christ Jesus."* (Philippians 2:1-5) (See Philippians 2:6-11)

The Lord had established my first love commitment to Him so now He was proceeding to order the rest of the priorities in my life — wife (home), church, school (career), etc. He showed me that love is all about commitment, accountability, and responsibility — to be accountable to my commitment to love (my wife and the people [ministry]). I was to love my wife as Christ loved the church, and gave Himself for it.

"Many profess unfailing love, but a faithful servant who can find?" (Proverbs 20:6)

I love building up relationships with people because the Lord gave me a relationship and life with Him in and through Jesus Christ who gave Himself for me. We are ministers of reconciliation, bringing the world to know the love of God. To build relationships we must build up Christ Jesus in one another, encouraging each person to realize the love of God and the good work the Lord has begun, is doing, and will complete in them (Philippians 1:6) and through them (Ephesians 2:10).

Diana and I were having so much fun together growing in the Lord and with each other. I am intense and she is playful and fun. What a great combination. In life the Lord puts people together to compliment each other and to add to each other in order to accomplish His purpose to His glory. May we never lose the joy of the Lord's presence and each other's presence in this lifetime. Relationships are the most important thing to God and should be to us.

"God so loved the world [people] *that He gave His only begotten Son* [Jesus Christ — God Himself come in the flesh] *that whoever* [anyone] *believes in Him* [Jesus Christ] *shall not perish but will have everlasting life."* (John 3:16 KJV)

RELATIONSHIPS WITH OTHERS

Satan hates relationships. He wants to destroy or pervert relationships. He wants relationships to be selfish, divided, having no joy or peace, unforgiving, envious, competitive, critical, rejected, showing partiality, insecure (people comparing and competing with each other), tearing self and others down, etc.

People who do not know the love of God or are not allowing the Lord's love to influence their life and behavior will fall prey to these Satanic devices. People apart from Jesus' love (whether believer or unbeliever) are users, cruel, hurtful, jealous, bitter, angry, striving, and selfishly thoughtless and uncaring of others feelings and lives.

God's favor and love on your life will create problems for you from people under the devil's influence. I was amazed at how unkind the other wives were to Diana when I came back to the campus. They did not include her or accept her. Some of my family did not accept her. They had their own issues. Sounds like playground behavior when you are a little child and children vie for attention, recognition, and identity. It was their loss to not enjoy and benefit from the gift of God in Diana's life. Everyone has such a gift. God created each of us to be a gift to the world. The expression "to know me is to love me" is very interesting. Will we take the time to know someone before we judge them?

If you know who you are (a child of God), how you are (loved by God), where you are (in the moment in the Spirit of the Lord [joyful and at peace with whoever]), and what you are about (advancing the love of God in the earth), you will not be concerned about doing selfish, immature, demonic behavior. If you do not know these things, you cause yourself and others pain by allowing the devil to use you.

All of my life, I have dealt with this kind of frightened, intimidated, jealous behavior whether in relationship with others towards me or in helping people to get free so they can have a blessed life. We people are so strange. God loves us in spite of us for His name's sake. That is how God taught me.

You just love people and go on about God's business, not taking other people's issues personally. The Lord and you are a majority. Jesus knew this and that is why He was not concerned or affected when the people and disciples rejected and abandoned Him, trying to figure out their own lives, loyalties, and commitment. Jesus knew the Father would not leave or forsake Him. (Hebrews 13:5-6)] He knew the Lord is His Helper and that He need not fear (absence of love) what men or women or little children, or the devil would do to Him.

"God's perfect love casts out all fear, for fear has torment." (1st John 4:18 KJV)

CHALLENGES TO WEDDED BLISS

When you live the single life, it is you and God. When you are married, it is you, God, and your spouse. I knew these things but I needed to cover, protect, and care for my wife as well. I needed to support and bring her along with me, not "everyone for themselves." We are family, a team.

I was trained in the counseling academics of marriage, but it is another thing when the fun starts to wane and the fire starts to lessen in your own life. In the first year of marriage God was blessing, and then the thief tried to destroy what God was doing. The test was on!

"Love always protects, always trusts, always hopes, always perseveres. Love never fails." (1st Corinthians 13:7-8)

The Lord had me on a "real" marriage seminar. You do not actually realize how selfish (or self-centered) you are until you get married. If you want your marriage to disintegrate, just start undermining it. The devil and everything in (and of) the world wants you to be unfaithful to God, yourself, and your spouse.

Husbands are to love their wives like they love themselves and as Christ loved the church. Wives are to respect and honor their husbands as to the Lord.

Unfaithfulness is not just running off with someone else. It is not fulfilling your commitment to God, yourself, and your spouse. It is neglecting your commitment to love, support, protect, respect, forgive, encourage, and care for your spouse and your marriage in the Lord.

We need to draw near to God and to each other. Circumstances will either draw you closer to God and each other or they will drive you apart, depending on what you do with your commitment to God, yourself and your spouse. When things get rough, you find out whether you are committed or not!

Diana had left her life as she knew it and had begun a new life and beginning with me and the Lord. May I never forget or neglect the privilege and trust that the Lord and Diana have given to me. I have such a blessed relationship with God and with her then — and in the following years with her, God, and the trust of the care of God's people.

How you take care of your wife and children is how you take care of God's people. The Lord does not want those caring for His people who cannot take care of their own life and household commitment. (1st Timothy 3:1-7; Titus 1:5-9)

You can go to all the counseling in the world, but without the Lord's help a blessed marriage cannot happen. I needed and still need supernatural help from God, and I sought Him earnestly because I did not know what to do. He gave me wisdom and knowledge as to how my wife, myself, and the marriage worked. (James 1; 1st Peter 3:7)

Fighting and strife broke out (Diana is woman and I am man), but power struggles ruin marriages. I tried to use the Word of God, but she thought I was manipulating her. "Take your scriptures and shove them" she would say in that first year. She would then search the scriptures to prove me wrong. The Lord would show her the truth. Eventually we made an agreement, not her will or my will be done, but God's will be done.

I was seeing and living what I saw happen in my parent's marriage when I was in high school. I hated it — the arguing and fighting, no peace or joy, no relationship. *"Beware lest a root of bitterness spring up and many be defiled."*

The Lord taught me that if you say or entertain negative thoughts about your spouse, you stab yourself in the back (an unfaithful betrayer working). Who in their right mind would want to do that?

She was not happy, and I knew curses were being sent against our marriage by the devil and those who did not want our marriage to last. The commitment and faith, hope, and love were being proved. I did not know what to do. It was out of my control. (I always thought I could get along with anyone — but now she did not want to get along with me.) What are you going to do? We were married. This is for life and you cannot make someone stay or love you.

Then the thoughts came: *Do I want this? Who is this woman?* (I learned about the monthly cycle.) I told her if she was so unhappy, she should go back home but "Don't let the door hit you on the way out and don't expect me to go running after you!" Then she or I would come back to our senses and seek God's and each others' forgiveness.

One time I was thinking she was carnal (not spiritual). The Lord said to me, "You are carnal for thinking that she is carnal. I have made her the way she is to My glory." I asked the Lord's forgiveness for not appreciating the way the Lord made her and worked through her as a compliment to what I do and as a joy to my life. Diana refreshes and warms people's hearts so I can share the Word.

Another time the Lord showed me that I was trying to make her into my image (of how she was to be) rather than His. He then told me, "Leave her alone (do not pressure her), I will take care of her as you love, respect, and honor." No negatives.

What the Lord was telling me is that He is the one who has begun the good work in her and He will finish it — (the same for God's people). (Philippians 1:6; Ephesians 2:10) I was simply to love her (1st Corinthians 13:1-8) and provide an environment of understanding and positive care and encouragement for her to become everything God wanted her to become through His Word, faith, hope, and love. (See Loving Your Spouse DVD Series.)

Diana came to me one day and said, "I always thought I was a submissive wife until you said 'No.' " (Ephesians 5:22-24; 1st Peter 3:1-6)

Following our honeymoon, she said. "I'm so happy. That was the best honeymoon I've ever been on!" I had to ask the question, "How many have you been on?" (She was thinking of something kind to say to me, which blessed me.)

Another time after the children were out of the home, she said, "If I've ever accomplished anything in life for the Lord, I know that I have raised two godly children who love and obey Him." (They are now raising our godly grandchildren.) (Psalm 128)

Now we begin each new day as if it were the first day of our marriage. Yesterday is gone. We seek to carry only the good over into the next day. *"Submit to one another as to the Lord."*

When first married and the power struggle was going on, the prayer was, "God, change my spouse." Now it is, "Thank you for my spouse." I don't point at her and say to God, "Forgive her" only to have her point at me and say, "Forgive him." We say, "Forgiveness!" Instead of arguing we both drop to our knees and pray (submit to God) and tell the devil to get out of our house.

We know now she is not the problem and I am not the problem. But at that time we thought differently. One night the Lord gave me a revelation in a dream about what was really happening between us.

In the dream, I saw what appeared to be a dark shadowy figure (a devil) which had grabbed Diana by the hair and was dragging her off into the forest. She was naked (not covered by my wavering commitment.)

At first, as I watched what was happening, I sat helplessly and did not seem to care. Suddenly, I stood to my feet with courage and shouted, "That is my wife and you can't have her!" I ran after her and beat up that devil. I covered her and took her in my arms, carrying her to safety.

A devil was attempting to drive us apart and ruin our marriage. We are not fighting people, but there were principalities of darkness (Ephesians 6:10-13) who wanted to steal, kill, and destroy. Jesus came that we might have abundant life and relationship.

As long as I was vacillating (being double minded — James 1:6-7) about whether I wanted to be married to Diana or just remain single the rest of my life (1st Corinthians 7:10-11, 15-17), the devil had access and power to steal and destroy (I do not believe in divorce. I believe in commitment and faithfulness — like Christ and the church).

Out of her ignorance of demonic ways, Diana was vulnerable and I was powerless because of my wavering commitment. Thank God for the manifestation of the Holy Spirit which exposed the devil's working. When I said, "That is my wife and you (devil) can't have her," I stood up for God and my commitment to my wife. The power and authority of God rose up in me and I beat that devil and then protected, covered, and cared for my wife. She is God's blessing to me, not a rottenness to my bones. (Proverbs 12:4) I asked Diana's forgiveness and she mine.

A UNITED FRONT

After hundreds and hundreds of counseling sessions, I was amazed how many people really do not want to be committed to their spouses, yet they call themselves God's people and ministers. This should not be so. You will not be able to be strong in the Lord in the evil day if there is no commitment. You will see few good days because you are unfaithful.

Following seminary graduation, the Lord was preparing both of us for a united front in meeting the people for the ministry that was before us. A united front is necessary to care for people whether it is a marriage, raising children, pastoring a church, or working a business.

Many married couples are not one in spirit. The Lord was making us one and we were learning to allow it to happen as we submitted first to the Lord and then to each other. The Lord taught me that I needed to include Diana in my life and the ministry.

Diana has always respected and honored the Lord and me in that she allows me the freedom to do what the Lord gives me to do. She trusts, prays, and encourages me that I hear the Lord. I know that I can always count on her to do what the Lord directs us to do. We are a team and getting better at it through hard work and God's grace.

She never has needed to be titled "co-pastor," yet for all these years she has faithfully, behind the scenes, taken care of me, the children, and the people of God. She jokes, "My office is the second stall on the left." The Lord honors her and it is an honor and a privilege to have her as my wife. (See her book titled, *My Pastor, My Husband*)

After seminary graduation we set off for our first ministry assignment together. It was a church in Southern California. As wonderful as the Lutheran church had trained me in the academics and practical discipline of ministry, our real Holy Spirit training was about to begin. A trial by fire.

"It is not by might or by power, but My Spirit, says the Lord Almighty." (Zechariah 4:6)

Jesus never entrusted himself to people, but only to the Father. The Lord was his source and guide determining his life and actions. Jesus never did or said anything that his Father in Heaven did not give him. He lived to please His Father and do His will.

A FIERY TRIAL

We were called, ordained, trained, and ready for action when we received a call to a small church in Southern California. Who would have thought that the next three years of ministry were to change our entire lives?

Diana and I arrived at this church with simple God expectations to bring the Lord's Word, love, and care of the people (for the Lord is coming soon). We wanted to see the Lord's best happen for the people. We love people because God loves us and we are thankful.

But like Moses, Jesus, Paul, and all the ministers of God came to and will come to realize — the care of the people is no easy job. Traditions and opinions of man, power plays, competition, comparison, selfishness, jealousy, strife, gossip, unbelief, and disobedience seem to surface when given opportunity. Some people and situations seem to give more opportunity.

We stepped into one of those situations. There had been five pastors in twelve years at this church. We believe in the Lord ordering our steps (Proverbs 3:5-6, Psalm 37:23) and looking back we know the Lord was shaping us for the ministry to which He had called us. Everything in our lives was to be tested — the call to the ministry, our love and commitment for the people; our faithfulness and obedience to God, health, etc.

The ministry is a noble calling, but like John the Baptist said, "No one can take to himself something that God has not given from heaven." (John 3:27) Many who have begun in the ministry are no longer there. Like marriage or any other commitment, we must sort out our motivations and reasons for what we are doing. If we do not, life and people will help us.

The Lord has given to us the opportunity over the years to love and care for many of the Lord's servants who have grown weary, disillusioned, and bitter because of what happened when they cared for the people. Others have fallen to females, fame, and pursuit of fortune. Because we have survived by God's grace and overcome these things, we can help those to overcome who are struggling. (2nd Corinthians 1:3-7) *Lord, help us all to be faithful to the end and receive Your crown of life.*

We must know and remember that the people are not the problem, but rather demonic influences using people who are not in the will of God (like people who persecuted Jesus, Paul, and Peter (Ephesians 6:12) etc. People with authority issues want to be in charge. Hurting people hurt. Abused people abuse. Prideful, selfish people create strife and contention. Bitter people bring in division. All have allowed demonic influence in their lives to affect others.

Without the Holy Spirit's supernatural ministry, God's will and purpose will not be accomplished and the minister will be worn out and beat up. So I learned! Except the Lord built the house [the ministry] they that labor, labor in vain, rising early and staying up late. "*Unless the Lord builds the house, its builders labor in vain. Unless the Lord watches over the city, the watchmen stand guard in vain.*" (Psalm 127:1)

There is man's church, and there is God's church, man-control or God-control. The two oppose each other. Where the Spirit of the Lord is there is liberty, unity, righteousness, peace and joy in the Holy Spirit. Where man is leading there is contention, partiality, division, striving, greed, and no move of God (a social club).

When the Lord is allowed to control by His Spirit and Word, there will be war (until man's control [demonic] is broken). This is why it has been said, "We had no problems in this church until people started witnessing about Jesus, praying for the sick, having Bible studies, and speaking in tongues." (Mark 16:15-18)

1st and 2nd Timothy, Titus, and 1st Peter 5:1-3 helped me to understand what I was about as a minister of God. Proverbs and Ecclesiastes gave me wisdom to deal with people and a perspective on life. (See *The Love Disciple* book).

One day a man said to me after service, "Pastor, I like the way you speak, but I didn't understand what you said." Being concerned that the people understand what I say, I researched what was said by reading the sermon reports the confirmands did each week, and listening to the tape, etc. Everyone understood what I said including the children. I asked the Lord, "Why doesn't this man, who is an 'elder' in the church, understand?" The Lord said, "He is not born again. Preach the gospel next week." I did so and he received the Lord and understood what I said. Just because someone is in church does not mean they are of God's Spirit.

Another day a man wanted to fight me in the parking lot. He said, "You have no right to talk about me and my family from the pulpit." Apparently the Holy Spirit had spoken through me about his family (a word of knowledge — 1st Corinthians 12). I had no knowledge of his situation, but God did. Another man in the crowd that had gathered asked, "Who here had the Lord talking through the pastor about you today?" Many in the crowd raised their hands. He then said to the other man, "If the Lord hits you between the eyes — fall down!" (He had no knowledge of falling down in the Spirit but it actually happened later, along with deaf ears hearing, people publically repenting of sins, and all the normal Holy Spirit signs and wonders that confirm God's Word. God's Word will expose who is who and what is what. (Hebrews 4:12)

There were people who told me, "Shut that book (the Bible); talk sense to us." I had to tell them the Word of God (His Truth) spoken in love so they could grow into all that the Lord wanted them to become and equip to do what He had prepared for them to do.

It is amazing how a few people can puff themselves up to be so important that they speak for "everyone else." A minister of God must not be afraid or compromise what the Lord has given him to say and do. You speak for God. Remember what Moses did when division tried to come through Miriam and the elders. He fell on his face and prayed. God delivered him, and the Lord will do the same for you. (Joshua 1:5-9) He did for me! (Isaiah 41)

There seemed to be no making peace with certain people who wanted to control the church. (The Lord should control the church.) They complained about this or that. They wanted more fellowship activities. I laid out a year of activities. Everyone else had a great time — but they never came to anything. Maybe that is why everyone else had a good time — but then how could I care and reach these other people (the shepherd's dilemma)?

"A shepherd who follows sheep steps in stuff." The Lord taught me to lead His way. For a period of several months, I lost all my strength. I only had enough strength to speak the Word on Sunday, otherwise I had to rest. The doctors said, "You are the perfect specimen of health." The care of the people had overwhelmed me. The Lord was showing me I could not minister on my own.

One day as I was resting, the Lord spoke to me, "Son, what are you doing?" I replied, "I'm killing myself working night and day about the ministry (people do not take into consideration the needs or time of the minister unless we set the boundaries). The Lord replied, "I've already saved the world. What are you doing? You only need to do what I (not the people or yourself) tell you to do — no more and no less."

The Lord then proceeded to teach me how to care for His people His way (See the *How to Help People* book, *Compassion*, *Dealing with People Pressure*, *God's Rest, The Helper's Handbook*).

I told the Lord, "Jesus only ministered three years," and He told me, "You are in the ministry for the long haul." *"Come to me you who are weary and burdened and I will give you rest. Take my yoke upon you and learn from me, for I am gentle and humble in heart, and you will find rest for your soul. For my yoke is easy and my burden is light."* (Matthew 11:28-30)

PRINCIPLES OF MINISTRY

(See the book of Timothy, Titus, and 1st Peter 5) (See also *The Love Disciple, Tips for Life,* and *Tips for Jesus' Disciples*):

1. Whatever you do, do it with all your heart in the name of Jesus to the glory of God.
2. Be an example.
3. Abide in faith, hope, and love — leading, not driving, God's people. Do not lord over the people entrusted to you.
4. Keep the Ten Commandments and obey God's Word and Spirit.
5. Love and care for people as one who must give an account to God. Ministry is a privilege and a trust. Relationship is a privilege and a trust.
6. You are not God, but God in you is the Lord of all — you represent Him to people through His Word. Ask whatever you will.
7. Praise the Lord and give thanks to God continuously.
8. Respect and honor God, authorities, and everyone.
9. Humble yourself under God's mighty hand — cast your cares on Him.
10. The Lord is the source of everything — spiritually, mentally, physically, financially, and in relationships.
11. Do not be argumentative. (2nd Timothy 2:24-26)
12. Study God's Word to show yourself a workman approved of God. Meditate on God's Word.
13. Be kind and friendly.
14. The Lord is with you. Stay close to Him.
15. Pray-pray-pray in understanding and in the Spirit. Spend time with God first, and then the people.
16. Ask God for wisdom. (James 1:5)

17. Have integrity in character and dealings with others. Pay your bills.
18. Do not use or abuse your position for personal gain or advantage.
19. Be faithful to the Lord and to the people. (1st Corinthians 4:1-5)
20. Lay down your life for the people; don't be a hireling.
21. Be thankful for the people (Philippians 1:3), and let the peace of God dwell and rule in your heart and mind.
22. Be a giver, not an opportunist, greedy for money. (1st Peter 5:3) Be eager to serve, not for recognition, reward, or compensation, but for God's glory.
23. Entrust self and ministry to God. You serve and please God. Serve people under the Lord's direction. (1st Peter 5:2)
24. Don't fear man which is a snare, nor seek man's recognition. Popularity is fickle. You will compromise God's Word and purpose, losing His blessing and ministry.
25. The measure of "greatness" in God's eyes is the measure of obedience and service to God, and His ministry to people.
26. When persecution comes (and it will if you are living, saying, and doing what God wants) do not take it personally. It is Jesus in you being persecuted, not you. (Matthew 10)
27. The Lord is more concerned about you and the people's growth in godly character and life through the Word and Spirit than He is about what you "accomplish" in life. Be more concerned that God is big in you and in the people rather than having a "big" ministry.
28. Avoid competition and comparison with other ministers and ministries. We are a team. Rather encourage and support one another. (1st Corinthians 3-4; 12)
29. Believe God for miracles — spiritually, mentally, physically, financially, and in relationships. Nothing is impossible to God or you in Him. (Matthew 17:20) He is true to His Word. (Numbers 23:19)

30. Know the Lord is with you and will never leave or forsake you so you do not have to fear devils or people. (Hebrews 13:5-6) You are working with God as a co-laborer.
31. Do not rejoice that you have authority over everything in Jesus' name. (It is good to know and to exercise the authority that the Lord has given to us!) However, rejoice that your name is written in the Book of Life. (Luke 10:19)
32. As you grow in the Lord, so will the people grow. The good work the Lord has begun in you, He will be faithful to perfect and complete. The Lord has begun and is doing His good work in you and in the people. Relax and enjoy what the Lord is doing in you and the people. (Philippians 1:6)
33. Have fun with the Lord, yourself, your family, and the people. Allow the Lord to occupy your time with gladness of heart. (Ecclesiastes 5:20)
34. Jesus said, "Push off the boat," and left the multitudes behind. He went to the mountains. Get your rest. Take a vacation. Let the Lord direct and order your time and ministry.
35. Take care of yourself and your family in the Lord. Then you will have a strong base of ministry to care for the people.
36. "My food is to do the will of Him who sent Me." (John 4:34) I come, O Lord, to do your will. (John 6:38) Do not worry about what you will eat, drink, or wear. Seek first the Kingdom of God and all these things will be added to you. (Matthew 6:31, 33) As we are about God's business, He will take care of whatever pertains to our life. (See 2nd Peter 1:2-11)
37. Avoid distractions (like making money, cares of the world, deceitfulness of riches, lust of other things, etc.) which take you away from what the Lord has called you to do (vision).
38. Believe that the Lord will supply whatever you need for the ministry He has called you (not someone else) to do (faithful helpers, provision [finance], equipment, facilities, etc.) It will be there when you need it. It is God's determination, not yours. After all, He makes all things beautiful in its time. (Ecclesiastes 3:11)

39. Always remember the humble beginnings when it was God and you! The tendency is to forget the Lord when He prospers and expands your path of influence. (Deuteronomy 8:11-18) If we are faithful with a little, the Lord will give increase. However, remember it is not self-effort or programs that determine the increase. The Lord has given to each of us an assignment in the Body. We must be faithful to do what He has given to us whether it is caring for one person or one million people.
40. Value and significance of ministry are not determined by size and wealth of ministry, but rather by faithfulness to what you are called to do.
41. Truth out of balance is heresy. Do not go beyond what is written. Many ministers of God have fallen because they were seeking some "new" revelation, insight, or knowledge (remember Eve in the garden) and strayed from balanced, sound doctrine and truth. "Knowledge puffs up, but love edifies (builds up)." (1st Corinthians 8:1-3 NKJV) Are we promoting the kingdom of God or self?
42. If what we are teaching and doing is not promoting faith, hope, and love in and for God and each other, it is unprofitable for life and ministry purposes.
43. We are stewards and caregivers of God's people. They are not ours. We all belong to the Lord. Just like a husband will present his family to the Lord someday, so we will present to the Lord the people of God entrusted to us for the Lord's care. (Hebrews 13:7, 13)
44. With God's anointing and favor will come misunderstanding and jealousy amongst other ministers and people who are operating in the flesh (competing and comparing) and the world, who do not want to see the kingdom of God prospering. Just love and forgive people and continue to do what the Lord has given to you. We are people, at different places of faith, hope, and love.
45. Your labor in the Lord is not in vain and the Lord will reward you. Together we will hear the Lord tell us "Well done, good and faithful servant (minister) of God. Come and receive My pleasures which I have prepared for you."

46. Equip the people for the work of the ministry. (Ephesians 4:12) They will not be concerned about their needs when they are ministering to others. Many ministers of God have fallen because they were not prepared for and sought after popularity, fame, and fortune. The presence, anointing, and wisdom of God are more important than the accolades of man and uncertain riches.
47. Make it your ambition to live a quiet life. (1st Thessalonians 4:11-12)
48. The Lord will give the vision, plan, policies, personnel, and provision for what He wants. It is important to make certain to let Him order the ministry.

Jesus was not in the ministry for himself, but to save us and to fulfill His Heavenly Father's desires. Jesus would not allow anyone to call him "good teacher," because there was no one "good" except His Father in heaven.

Jesus did not need to be the center of attention for his own benefit or personal gain. The Lord made Jesus the center of attention that whoever believes in and acknowledges Jesus as their Lord will be saved and have life forever with God.

HOLY SPIRIT MANIFESTATIONS

After several months of this "unexplained" lack of strength, through which the Lord taught me how to minister and rely upon His strength and not my own, He told me, "Go have the elders anoint and lay their hands on you, and you will be healed." (James 5:14) So I called together the people who helped me, and we did what the Lord said to do, believing the Lord to do what He said He would do.

No one in the church or myself had ever done such a thing, but there it was in James 5:13-16. From boyhood I had always been taught that what the Lord says is the Truth and if we do what He says, He will do what He says.

Yes, the Lord did what He said He would do when we did what He said to do. He healed me! Then He began to heal everyone in the congregation. Healings and miracles began to happen as we believed for them to happen. The Holy Spirit began doing things we were not even believing for.

An openness to the Lord allowed a climate for the Lord to do whatever He wanted to do. He started sending people to us who were open to the Holy Spirit. They seemed rather strange, with their conversations about speaking in tongues, but I enjoyed their love and enthusiasm for the Lord. I had never heard about or seen these kinds of things in my church training and background.

Although the Word of God talks about this (1st Corinthians, chapters 12-14; Jude 20; Acts 2:4; 10:46, 11:15-17, 19:1-7) the church I was raised in never spoke one way or the other about this tongue-talking stuff. Yet, I was raised as a child to believe that whatever the Lord says in His Word is true and is to be obeyed and practiced. I guess we just had not discovered (were ignorant of) or just avoided certain sections of the scriptures (disobedient and unbelieving).

When the Lord wants you to know or do something, He will keep putting it in your face. One day as I was sitting at my desk, the Lord said to me, "Son, you are loaded with spiritual pride!" (To me this was the worst of all sins, being religious.) I replied, "Father, how so?" He said, "You are determining what I will give to you, rather than allowing Me to determine what I will give to you." (See *Holy Spirit* booklet)

The Lord is always right. I had been telling people, "If God has given to you this speaking in tongues, that's great. It is in the Bible, but use it in an orderly manner. As for me, the Lord has not given it to me and uses me in other ways." The Lord has used me since I was a little boy in many ways that neither I nor my pastors understood. But this tongue speaking was to me not useful (my ignorance) and I really did not think I needed it (my pride).

I was not seeking understanding (1st Corinthians 12:1) (the Lord does not want us ignorant), nor was I seeking to operate in spiritual (supernatural) workings. The Lord says to desire them for His ministry purposes (1st Corinthians 14:1).

I was full of spiritual pride when all along I thought I was being a good, balanced pastor. The Lord taught me years later what a balanced minister of God is to be. He said, "My children desire to be like Me. Some think that means being full of the fruit of the Spirit (God's character — Galatians 5:22-26 — truth and integrity). Others think that means being full of the gifts of the Spirit (1st Corinthians 12 — supernatural workings). If my children are to be like Me, they must have the fruit of My Spirit and operate in the gifts of My Spirit." To be balanced in God is to have God's character and His spiritual, supernatural manifestations (John 14:12-14) like Jesus.

The Lord wanted me to have (and was developing) His character and supernatural workings in me so I could fulfill His calling and purpose to His glory. I needed to allow the supernatural elements of the Holy Spirit to be added to God's character in me.

I asked the Lord's forgiveness for my spiritual pride and ignorance and He made me even more open to Himself and His ways. Eagerly desiring His spirituals, and seeking understanding on the Holy Spirit and His ways (see Holy Spirit book), the Lord made Himself, people, and materials available to me. He used them to encourage and explain His Truths to me, as Aquila and Pricilla helped Apollos and Paul, and as Jesus learned in the wilderness. The Lord will equip us with what we need if we make ourselves available to be equipped by His Spirit.

I would read, *"Pray without ceasing."* After a few hours I would run out of things to pray for, but praying in the Holy Spirit (in tongues),

I can pray the will of God without ceasing. On one such day as I was praying as usual, I began speaking in another language which I did not know. Immediately after these words came out of my mouth, "Hosanna, Hosanna, glory to God in the highest glory. Blessed are they who come in the name of the Lord." This was not normal for me. Later I found out that I was operating in the ministry gift of tongues and interpretation.

This was different from the prayer tongue that I was using now as an adult, speaking it to God. (1st Corinthians 14:2) (As a child I would sing little songs in what I thought were made-up words, and great peace would come upon me. Our church would pray every week, "Lord, fill us with the Holy Spirit.") Now I know I was filled with the Holy Spirit, singing in the Spirit.

The next week as I was reading the Lord's Word, the Holy Spirit directed me to Matthew 23:39. Jesus says, *"For I tell you, you will not see me again until you say, 'Blessed is He who comes in the name of the Lord.' "*

From that day on miraculous Holy Spirit things and divine appointments increased. One day a man came to my office. He was crying. According to his account, when he would drive by a school he would immediately go to the bar to get drunk. However, this time something led him to my office. Apparently, during World War II, he had bombed a school, killing over 300 children. The guilt was destroying his life.

The Holy Spirit will guide our words and actions, if we ask. I inquired, "Have you asked the Lord's forgiveness?" He said he had many times. We did so again. "Did the Lord forgive you?" I responded. He said, "Yes." Then I said, "You now need to forgive yourself." When he did, freedom and joy filled him. I then cursed the guilt off of him in Jesus' name. He was free and rejoiced in the Lord.

CASTING OUT DEVILS

The Holy Spirit was continuing to instruct me about His workings. The next area He taught me was the casting out of devils. (See *Satan's Defeat* book) If I had known about this years before, I would not have been sick so much. We did not know about spirits of infirmity. How do you know if a person has a sickness or disease or a spirit of infirmity? This question is usually in response to my statement, "You can pray for the sick all day, and they will not get better if they have a spirit of infirmity. You must cast out the spirit."

Unless the Holy Spirit shows you, you do not know whether it is a spirit or a sickness and disease. Understand, the demon spirit does not know whether you know it is there or not. Say, "Whatever is not of the Lord Jesus leave their body (or mind) in Jesus' name! And whatever is of the Lord Jesus come to them in Jesus' name!" The result is whatever is not of God (devils and sickness) will leave and what is of God will come to them (healing and deliverance).

In my first encounter with demonic deliverance, the Lord walked me through it. (See how to cast out and understand devils in the *Satan's Defeat* book.) I had read about deliverance in the Word of God, and that the Lord had given us authority over all the power of the devil (Luke 10:18-21), but I had never seen it or been a part of it.

I can understand why the Lord Jesus told the disciples to rejoice more that their names were written in the Book of Life because casting out devils and healing the sick in the name of Jesus and the authority of God is tremendously awesome! To this day I love to see the Lord glorify Himself. What a privilege to be able to use the name of Jesus and to know that all heaven and earth is moving to God's glory when we speak that name. (John 14:12-14, Matthew 28:18-19)

In my earlier days the Lord's angels would deal with some tall, dark, shadowy presences which would come to me. (Angels appeared as pillars of light or shooting light beams — devils shriveled and left.) Now the Lord wanted me to take authority over these things.

It was in my second encounter with demonic deliverance that the Lord showed me an exciting truth. Many people are afraid and ignorant of spiritual things. We do need to be aware of the devil, but not be afraid of him.

As a minister of the Lord, we must always be aware that while the Lord is building His kingdom, the devil is working, trying to tear it down. But always remember what is intended for evil, the Lord will turn it around for good. (Genesis 50:20)

In this second encounter I was ministering to a paraplegic man that we had led to the Lord Jesus, baptized, filled with the Holy Spirit, and he spoke in tongues. His wife had been sent to us when our organist told us that she would no longer play for the ministry. (The organist had been set up by some others who were trying to control and work against the ministry.) I thanked her for her time of faithful service. She looked at me and said, "Is that all you have to say?" I said, "Yes."

As a minister of God you must not let people control you. The Lord will supply what you need when you need it (proper people, plans, policies, provision). Make no mistake, we need what the Lord supplies, not a counterfeit which will bring trouble. The Lord is our source. Be patient for what He has.

The next day God sent me His pianist. She accompanied us in the ministry, leading people in spiritual worship for over 25 years before she went home to the Lord. (God's provision.) This woman was legally blind. (Before Christ was in her life she had pricked her eyes with pins while in a drunken state), but as she played to the Lord in a state of grace and forgiveness, the Lord healed her, enabling her to see the smallest print.

While I was ministering to her husband, I asked the Lord, "What is causing this bedsore?" The Lord said, "A spirit of death." I did not know that to a paraplegic a bedsore often means death. In the name of Jesus, I commanded, "Spirit of death, get off him!"

When I did so, the man sat up in his bed. (Paraplegics cannot sit up.) Then he stood up. (Like Peter stood on the water until he saw what he was doing.) As he started to slump I caught him and sat him on the edge of the bed. The Lord then said, "Put the blood of Jesus over him." I said, "The blood of Jesus covers you."

When I said this, something threw the man across the room. As he lay on the floor, a devil spoke out of his mouth, "Have you come to torment me before the time?" It was not talking to me, but to Jesus! I realized I do not need to be afraid. It is Jesus, not me, doing this when I speak His name. The Lord is with us in the ministry. (John 14:12-14)

One night in a dream I saw one of the church members lying in bed very sick. I saw a spirit come on her. The family was all around the bed. Walking up to the front door, I walked in, went to the bedroom, and cast the devil out, and the woman was healed and got out of bed.

The next day I went to the family's house. Walking through the front door, I went to the bedroom. The family was around the bed. In Jesus' name I cast out the devil, and the woman was healed and got out of the bed just like the Holy Spirit had shown me.

WHEN OPPOSITION ARISES

As a minister of God, we must live peaceably with others, as much as lies within us. Walk in love and not be quarrelsome. (Romans 12:9-21, 2nd Timothy 2:24-26) However, you cannot compromise the truth. Up to this point in life I had thought that there was no one who I could not get along with.

A true love test was about to happen. You never really learn to love the way Christ Jesus loved until you have an enemy. Yet Jesus never viewed people as enemies, but rather as those whom He was to give His life for that they might have life with God (true ministry and service to God and man). (Romans 12:9-21, 5:9-11)

We cannot love people and the praise of people more than we love the Lord. True peace does not come without war. A commitment must be made first to God and then to the people. The Lord must be our first love before self, ministry (others) family, or anything. (Matthew 10)

When the presence and power of God began to manifest, I wanted to draw near to the Lord even more. Like Paul, I was forsaking all to know Jesus and the power of His resurrection. With this there is a cost — the fellowship of His sufferings and persecution. (Philippians 3:7-11; Mark 10:29-31)

God's kingdom is about righteousness, peace and joy in the Holy Spirit. (Romans 14:17-18) The truth and justice of the Lord's Word cannot be watered down or compromised if we are to receive the Lord's results for His people. We must live, speak, and do what the Word of God says, holding forth to the people the truth and example of Christ Jesus as we prepare for His return.

What creates the opposition is the passion and intensity of one's conviction for the love of God, the Word of God, and the love of the people to see them know and do the will of God. Where there is lukewarmness, unbelief, disobedience, and apathy, there is no persecution.

If you seek the honor and favor of men, you cannot have the praise and honor of God. Yet, if you honor the Lord, He will give you honor and favor with those who honor Him.

Jesus said, *"Who is my mother, brothers, and sisters? Those who hear and do the will* [the Word] *of Him who sent me."* (Luke 8:21) His family thought Jesus had gone crazy.

Compassion is not compromise. Compromise has no power because it is divided truth. Compassion has power (Matthew 20:34) because the truth is not divided. One cannot serve two masters. Truth cannot be watered down by tradition and the opinions of men (Matthew 15:3-9), feelings, fears, and ambitions for people or self (one's own life).

People can either be used of the Lord or by the devil. *"Many profess unfailing love, but a faithful servant who can find?"* The Lord does not change. People do change when they get their thoughts off the Lord and His purpose. Peter told Jesus that He did not have to go to the cross because Peter wanted Jesus to stay with him. Jesus loved both Peter and Judas who rejected and betrayed Him. We love people no matter what they say or do to us.

We people are truly like sheep that need a shepherd. Thank God for Jesus. We shepherds need to follow Jesus. Ministers of God need to lead God's people by serving and caring for them under the direction of the Holy Spirit. Loving them like Christ has loved and forgiven you – blessing, not cursing. Ministry that is not for personal gain, honor, or privilege, but with a genuine care for the people and a love for the Lord and His church.

When the kingdom of God is forcefully advancing, opposition will arise, as it has throughout church history. Those who will be godly will be persecuted. Do not take it personally. (Matthew 10) It is Jesus being persecuted, not you. Jesus says, "Bear up in God under hardship and praise Him, and bless, do not curse."

During this time of my life (and later times, for persecution comes in cycles), my family disowned me for "breaking the faith of the fathers."

People in the congregation who had personal issues, authority issues, and control issues were creating strife and division. The church denomination I had been raised in and trained by did not support their ministry. Other ministers in the denomination would not talk to me, but were talking about me. It seemed like everyone except Diana, my wife, had left. I thank the Lord for His faithfulness through her. Job's wife told him, *"Are you still holding on to your integrity? Why don't you just curse God and die."* (Job 2:9)

In times like these, I know to draw near to the Lord who will not leave or forsake me. Therefore I can boldly say, *"The Lord is my helper, I will not fear what man can do to me."* (Hebrews 13:5-6, Joshua 1:5, Psalm 91) In regard to relationship, I was learning about the safe place in God. Do not get disturbed, hurt, or bitter at people and life. (Always remember: What the thief intends for evil the Lord will turn to good if we set our heart on Him and do what He says to do.) The Lord gave me Psalm 121:1-2 — *"I will lift up my eyes to the hills, from whence cometh my help. My help cometh from the Lord..."* Another promise was Isaiah 30:19-21.

At times in our lives the Lord seems to remove all the sources that we have trusted or leaned to so we will go to Him as our source and strength, joy and crown. When we have received from Him, then He will return to us what He has prepared for us.

The apostle Paul said that we need to daily die to self and bring this body (mind) under subjection to our new spirit in Christ. Some days we act more spiritual than others, depending on what we are allowing to go on within and around us.

One day I was reading in the Psalms where David was telling the Lord to strike down his enemies. At that moment it sounded like something I wanted to pray. Before I could pray it, however, the Holy Spirit checked me, saying, "Son, David was wrong." (Just because someone says something in the Bible does not mean that is what the Lord wants us to say or think.)

The Lord went on to refer me to Matthew 5:43-48, *"Behold, I show to you a better way," "Love your enemies and pray for them who despitefully use and persecute you, that you may be sons of your Father in heaven..."* If you only love those who love you, what reward will you get?' I decided to pray a blessing on them.

A LOVE TEST

Another time the Lord gave me Proverbs 16:7: *"When a man's ways are pleasing to the Lord, He makes even his enemies live at peace with him."*

This verse haunted me for awhile. I could not get away from it. The Holy Spirit was revealing to me that I really did not like or love these people and would rather not have them around. I asked the Lord to forgive me and I forgave them, seeking to love them as I am loved! They were acting like devil children rather than God's children — selfish, rebellious liars, divisive, and undermining people's faith in God and myself as their pastor. They would disrupt services saying things like, "Don't open that book (the Bible); talk sense to us!" or "That's not Lutheran!" "You are not of God," etc.

The Lord has always taught me that He is not interested in my opinion or anybody else's opinion about anything. He is only interested that His ministers speak His Word (Truth) so people can grow into all He intends in person and deed. (Ephesians 4:11-16)

The Lord said to me in the pulpit one day, "Son, you can speak My Word (the Bible) and it not be My Word." (What the Lord was saying was that you can choose to speak on any subject or scripture in the Bible, but it may not be the Word the Holy Spirit wants said at that particular moment. The Holy Spirit word for that moment is the word the Lord confirms with signs and wonders following. (See *Power* booklet)

I was their pastor and I was called to be faithful to them and love and care for them until they moved on or I moved on. The Lord told me, "You will not be moved by man, but I will move you when it is the time." A small group attempted to move me out, but could not. The Lord built a new working of people which they could not influence. This confounded them.

He told me, "This week I will do a major work of My Spirit in this place." All excited, I stepped into the pulpit that Sunday only to find thirty-two people in attendance. (I think that was one of the few times I have ever counted the people. The Lord brings who He wants us to share with and to care for (John 6:37-40) nor will we turn anyone away.) The funds for the ministry doubled, and the Lord cleaned the house.

Again, what is intended for evil, the Lord will turn around for good to God's glory. The people who were being used and abused by the devil through ignorance, religious tradition, and pride left the church thinking, *If we leave and stop giving to the ministry, Pastor will fail.* The Lord gave me a word. (Read Isaiah 41:9-20)

What I discovered was that they really did not want me to love and care for them, nor to bring them God's Word. They wanted to run the church (be a social club and be important). I stood in the way of having what they wanted. I guess that is why they had five pastors in twelve years. We are known by the "fruit" or the track record of our life — the Lord is the judge.

THE LORD'S CHURCH VS. MAN'S CHURCH

This is not what the Lord's church is to be about. It is Holy Ground in which a holy God is making Himself a holy people to worship Him and advance His good news of salvation in Jesus to the uttermost parts of the earth. The kingdom of God is not about the minister or the people. It is to be all about Jesus Christ as the Lord of lords. His Word and Truth. To Him be the glory, power, and dominion forever and ever. Amen!

When church is about the minister or the people, we have problems. *"Without pride there is no contention,"* Paul said. *"So then, men ought to regard us as servants of Christ and as those entrusted with the secret things of God. Now it is required that those who have been given a trust must prove faithful. I care very little if I am judged by you or by any human court; indeed, I do not even judge myself. My conscience is clear, but that does not make me innocent. It is the Lord who judges me. Therefore judge nothing before the appointed time; wait till the Lord comes. He will bring to light what is hidden in darkness and will expose the motives of men's hearts. At that time each will receive his praise from God.* (1st Corinthians 4:1-5)

"Now, brothers, I have applied these things to myself and Apollos for your benefit, so that you may learn from us the meaning of the saying, 'Do not go beyond what is written.' Then you will not take pride in one man over against another. For who makes you different from anyone else? What do you have that you did not receive? And if you did receive it, why do you boast as though you did not?" (1st Corinthians 4:6-7)

God's church is not about how many people are coming, nor is it about money, fame, and popularity. The minister of God who is distracted by these things will not have favor with God and will lose favor with man. We are to be faithful and obedient to be, say, and do what the Lord has given each of us. We are not to compete with each other.

Rather, we are to encourage and strengthen one another. We are all a part (together) of God's team to God's glory.

Religious traditions and man's teaching (opinions) divide and distinguish one group from another, separating the Body of Christ. This is why we have not arrived to "unity in the faith" even though people say there may be "unity in the Spirit." (See Ephesians 4:1-16)

"There is one body and one Spirit — just as you were called to one hope when you were called — one Lord, one faith, one baptism; one God and Father of all, who is over all and through all in all." (Ephesians 4:4-5) If this is the case, why do ministers of God in the Body of Christ let the church become so divided? God's church and kingdom is not divided, like the Lord is not divided — There is but one God.

If the Holy Spirit is the teacher, why is He teaching us different things — about the same topic? Or is it that today (and over the ages) people have interpreted the Word of God (which was divinely inspired [2nd Peter 1:12-2:22]) not by the Holy Spirit but rather by their own understanding, unbelief, and teachings? Then they passed it down over the ages, whether true or false.

Jesus is coming back, and we need to be in unity in Spirit and in the faith. The Word of God has only one interpretation and one meaning by the one Holy Spirit who is teaching us. I was accused of not being a "Lutheran," and yet Luther said, "Let no man call himself a Lutheran or a papist, for neither Luther nor the pope has died for your sins." Luther was a Christian, not a Lutheran or a Catholic. (Also see: 1st Corinthians 3:1-4:21)

Scripture is to interpret itself. This was one of the principles of the Reformation. What does the Word say? Do not add to it or take away from it. *"Holy Spirit give us understanding, revelation, and faith to believe and receive what His words of spirit and life say. This will cause us to receive the divine nature of God and fulfill what He has called and chosen us to in Christ Jesus."* (2nd Peter 1:1-11)

The Catholic apologists wrote about the Reformation movement, "You say you are Bible, Bible, nothing but the Bible, but when it comes to the issue of God's Holy Sabbath [7th day], which you know was changed by papal decree [to Sunday], you have not changed it back. Why then don't you observe all the other papal decrees?" (Document from *The Lord's Day* booklet).

The reason God's holy fourth commandment — the 7th day Sabbath — was not changed by the reformers was they felt it would harm the acceptance of the Reformation (man's politics). In addition, the practice of infant baptism was changed by some of the reformers, but not by all.

History has revealed the evolution of teaching, tradition, and the resulting beliefs or lack of belief. The Formula of Concord (one of the founding declarations of the Reformation) states that when practices of the church (liturgies, forms of worship, etc.) are given more importance than the commandments of God, they are to be considered adiofera (to be of no matter) and done away with.

The Lord says, *"My people are destroyed for lack of knowledge. Because you have rejected knowledge, I also will reject you from being priests for Me; because you have forgotten the law of your God, I also will forget your children. The more they increased, the more they sinned against Me; I will change their glory into shame. They eat up the sin of My people; they set their heart on their iniquity. And it shall be; like people, like priests. So I will punish them for their ways, and reward them for their deeds."* (Hosea 4:6-9 NKJV)

The Lord is saying that His people are being destroyed because they do not have knowledge of God and His ways. Why? — Because the ministers have rejected the knowledge of the Lord and His Spirit's ways. They broke faith and unity with God.

KNOWING AND GROWING IN THE LORD

Hosea 4:6-9 is Old Testament, but in the New Testament, there is no excuse for the minister or the people. All of God's children are ministers and responsible to grow in the Lord through His Word by the Holy Spirit. The apostles, prophets, evangelists, pastors, and teachers are called to equip the saints for the work of the ministry. (Ephesians 4:11-16)

If the "five fold" ministry is doing its job, the people will know the Lord, His ways, and be equipped to be about His business. They will be blessed and not lack for any good thing. The people need to be taught the Word of the Lord (faith, hope, and love), not man's opinions or traditions, which Jesus says are vain and empty. (Matthew 15:3-9)

It has been said by Jesus that a student cannot be greater than his teacher. This is a matter of honor for the one who taught you. But it has also been said that a student can only rise to the understanding and faith of the teacher.

Jesus is our teacher and example. *Lord, I believe, help me to live, believe, and work the works of God as you did.* (John 14:12-14)

This means that if the teacher is not growing and advancing in Christ Jesus, the student will not grow either. You teach and live what you know and believe. If you do not know (and I don't mean knowledge "about" which puffs up) God, you have no relationship (love builds up – 1st Corinthians 8:1-3) with God. The man who loves God is known by God and knows God's ways.

We have not arrived yet, but we are pressing ahead to the mark of the high calling of God which is ours in Christ Jesus. (Philippians 3)

This is why it is so important that we do our best to present ourselves to God as one approved, a workman who needs not be ashamed and who correctly handles the word of Truth (through study, faith, and obedience). (2nd Timothy 2:11-26) The Lord will help us if we humble ourselves before Him. (Read 1st and 2nd Timothy) (See also, *Love Disciple*, and *So You Want to Be A Minister* books)

For unity in the faith to happen we must evaluate what we believe, how we came to believe it, and why we believe it. Paul instructed Timothy, *"Be diligent in these matters; give yourself wholly to them, so that everyone may see your progress. Watch your life and doctrine closely. Persevere in them, because if you do, you will save both yourself and your hearers."* (1st Timothy 4:15-16) (Read 1st Timothy 4:11-14)

We all need to be progressing in the Lord. As I was progressing in the Lord, the Lord taught me that it is not about what I or anyone else believe or do not believe that matters (although that will be what determines what I have — *"Be it done to you according to your faith"*). What matters is what the Lord says! I must believe, receive, and act upon what He says, not what I or anybody else thinks about things.

The Lord is not a man that He should lie or change His mind. Has He not said it and will He not do it? (Numbers 23:19)

The Lord had me meditate on this verse on two different occasions (once for 60 days and another time for 90 days). He wanted me to know that He means to do what He says He will do. The Holy Spirit told me during one of these times, "It is impossible that the impossible (what people consider impossible) not happen when you act upon My Word." I asked the Lord, "Why all the negatives?" He replied, "Because people are negative. All things are possible when you act (believe) on my Word!" (Matthew 19:26, Matthew 17:20-21)

I noted that if I really believed, I had to act on God's Word for the results to happen. People who have been taught that the Lord does what He wants when and if He wants to do it (that was what I had been taught) are sure going to miss it. They will always be waiting at the pool and never receive until they believe. Jesus said, "Act on your healing." (John 5:8) (See *Victory* book)

Because the Lord had me looking at His Word and not what I had been taught about His Word (and I was asking the Holy Spirit to teach me and show me Truth in Jesus' name) (John 16:12-13), I began to understand the Lord and His ways from His perspective rather than from man's understanding. (Read Matthew 13:11-17; Ephesians 1:17-23))

Jesus said it well. *"Leave them, they are blind guides. If the blind lead the blind, both will fall into a pit."* (Matthew 15:14) *"You are in error because you do not know* [understand from God's perspective] *the Scriptures or the power of God."* (Matthew 22:29) (See Matthew 23 where Jesus was talking with religious leaders) *"I have much to say to you, more than you can now bear."* (John 16:12)

"Not everyone can accept this word, but only those to whom it has been given." (Matthew 19:11) Let those who have ears to hear, hear what the Spirit of the Lord says. (Matthew 11:15)

"Now to Him who is able to do far more exceedingly abundantly above all that we ask or think, according to the power that works in us, to Him be the glory in the church." (Ephesians 3:20-21) The Lord showed me that I was not asking for enough.

THE HOLY SPIRIT AND THE WORD

Just as David inquired of the Lord, I began to ask Him what to ask for and how to do things. (James 1:3-8; Jeremiah 33:3) As I read the Word, the Lord showed me more things to ask for. I asked for the hearing ear and the instructed tongue so I could hear the Lord clearly and then speak what He wanted me to say for His purpose to be accomplished.

(Isaiah 50:4) I asked for wisdom to lead God's people in a way pleasing to Him, like Solomon did.

Jesus said to the church people, *"You study diligently the scriptures because you think that by them you possess eternal life. These are the scriptures that testify about me, yet you refuse to come to me to have life."* (John 5:39-40) This is a proof passage used in catechisms to teach the children about the importance of reading the Bible. It is not even talking about that. What it is saying is that you can read and know what the Bible says and miss the entire meaning and purpose of what it is about. There should be a living relationship through faith and obedience with a loving Lord who will love and save us and transform us into His divine nature for His glory, and escape from the corruption of the world. (2nd Timothy 3:14-17; 2nd Peter 1:2-5)

Jesus says, "My Words are Spirit and life." (John 6:63-64; Hebrews 4:12) Many of the disciples considered what He said hard and could not accept what He said so consequently they left Him to go back to their old belief system which they felt comfortable with. (John 6:60-70)

Many people today try to make the scriptures conform to their traditions and beliefs. Rather than approaching God's Word to ask and allow the Holy Spirit to receive truth, they think they already know truth and try to make God's Word say what they want it to say (or do not even look at it) to fit their beliefs and lifestyle. Then they gather together with people of like faith or unbelief to confirm their thoughts. Hence, we have many brands of Christianity today, each thinking they have all the truth and not accepting that they may not be open to the truth that others may have honestly by the Holy Spirit, or even know that there is such truth because they never searched the scriptures, or they interpreted it according to their unbelief.

Realizing this, I noticed that while I was raised in a church, trained in parochial school, high school, college, seminary, and pastored in a church that believed in infant baptism (and I was infant baptized),

I was accepted by that group. When the Holy Spirit revealed to me through the Word of God that one must repent, believe in Jesus and then be baptized (no infant could do this) (See *Water Baptism* booklet), then I was not accepted by them. Other groups accepted me, and I was then baptized in fulfillment of all righteousness. (Matthew 3:15)

When the Holy Spirit through the Word of God revealed to me about the infilling of the Holy Spirit, speaking in tongues, casting out devils, healing the sick, then I was no longer accepted by those groups. However, other groups accepted me who believed in healing. (Mark 16:14-20)

When the Holy Spirit revealed to me by the scriptures and by history that the 7th day Sabbath (the 4th commandment) was changed by man and not by God (See *The Everlasting Gospel* and *The Lord's Day* books), then I was not accepted by all of the other groups. Even the groups that believe in this did not accept because I believed in the other Holy Spirit things. Tradition has so blinded many that they will not even consider looking at something else. I want to know the Truth.

Praise the Lord! The Lord accepted me for believing, acting on, and teaching these things. Like Jesus said, "Those who love the Father love me, and I love them." Truth is Truth. The Lord is progressive. All who open their hearts and minds to His Truths in His Word will all become one in spirit and the faith (Ephesians 4:12-16) before His return. If we put all the truth which is in the different groups, we would have the belief and practice of the early apostles.

Even about Jesus' return there exist different beliefs over which people have separated: pre-tribulation, during tribulation, post-tribulation. This I know: there will be a return of the Lord Jesus and all who love and live for Him and His appearing are going to be with Him forever. We need to be found ready. We will all be together forever. So why not enjoy the Lord and each other together now, not just in lip service but in true devotion one to another? Alleluia.

"According to your faith will it be done to you," Jesus said. (Matthew 9:29) Whatever is not done out of faith is sin. Many people profess faith in this or that, but if they do not practice and follow what they believe, what good is it to them? (Romans 14:22-23; Philippians 3:15-16; 1st Corinthians 14:36-40)

SUBMIT TO GOD, HONOR THE AUTHORITIES

All of my life I have sought to honor and be faithful to the Lord and the authorities which He has placed in my life. (Exodus 20:12; Romans 13:1-5; 1st Peter 2:13-25; Hebrews 13:17) A minister of the Lord must learn to be under authority if one is to be an authority of quality. All authority comes from God and is here for our good. The Lord will use authorities to accomplish His purpose in our lives.

Jesus always honored the teachers' authority in His life. When brought before Pilate, he acknowledged that Pilate would have no authority over him except His Father in heaven had given it to him. Jesus submitted himself to the will of God, not resisting the authorities, but trusting that His life was in His Father's hands. (1st Peter 2:13-25)

Daniel in the lion's den; Shadrach, Meshach, and Abednego in the fiery furnace; and Jesus at the cross were all there at the hands of the authorities. They had no rebellion or opposition to God's will (which is witchcraft, disrespect, or dishonor in their hearts towards the authorities). (Daniel 3, 6)

Although the apostles must obey God rather than man (Acts 4 and 5), they submitted themselves to the Father who judges justly, with no disrespect towards the authorities in their lives because they trusted and knew their lives were in God's hands. The Lord would be honored whether in their life or their death and His purpose be accomplished to His glory. The Lord be praised!

The glory and blessing of God are on you when you are persecuted for doing the will of God. (1st Peter 4:13-19) (See *Loving Witness* and *Glory Crown* books) Rebellion and disrespect are not of God. The devil uses these things to get us out of the will of God like he was. We need to pray for the authorities in our lives, bless and be a blessing to them. (1st Timothy 2:1-4; Hebrews 13:7, 3:17) Although our kingdom is not of this world, we are in this world and need to be a witness for Jesus so people will be saved. Honor God and the authorities. Resist the devil.

"Humble yourselves, therefore, under God's mighty hand, that he may lift you up in due time. Cast all your anxiety on him because he cares for you. Be self-controlled and alert. Your enemy the devil prowls around like a roaring lion looking for someone to devour. Resist him, standing firm in the faith, because you know that your brothers throughout the world are undergoing the same kind of sufferings. And the God of all grace, who called you to his eternal glory in Christ, after you have suffered a little while, will himself restore you and make you strong, firm and steadfast. To him be the power for ever and ever. Amen. (1st Peter 5:6-11)

People will persecute you for the following reasons:

1. Ignorance, pride, or prejudice
2. Religion (fleshly) — a form of godliness which denies the power of godliness. Man's traditions and teachings put before God's Truth and ways.
3. Personal Conviction — your light (Jesus) has shown into their darkness.
4. Different beliefs (scripture and practice) about spiritual things
5. Jealousy and envy
6. Personal interests (position, power, and money) are threatened
7. The Word of God exposes their life and style

"Beware lest a root of bitterness springs up amongst you and many be defiled. (Hebrews 12:14-15) *From whence come quarrels and fightings among you? It comes from your own lust. You kill and covet. You want something and cannot have it so you fight for it."* (James 4:1-3)

HUMILITY AND FAITHFULNESS

Always remember that what is intended for evil, the Lord will turn for good. Sometimes people will not let go of what the Lord has *not* given them. The devil takes advantage of this situation. You do your best to work things out and communicate. Sometimes people will seek and yield to the Lord's wisdom and other times they will not.

In hundreds of sessions with people, I have discovered that one spouse will tell you one thing. The other will tell you something different. When they both sit down together, they say something even different. And the truth is usually something else.

Division always occurs because people refuse to humble themselves, seek God's face and forgiveness, forgiving one another. We are a team and God's ministers of reconciliation, but when we think more highly of ourselves than we ought, we miss the grace of God. (See *Loving Kindness* and *The Kindness Factor* books)

Man's ways of handling this situation is for one spouse or the other to leave. Power plays (the devil loves this) develop, trying to prove one is right and the other is wrong. Gossip, fault-finding, lying, slander, confusion, and every evil work result, causing people to choose sides. Bitterness spreads, defiling more people. Others withdraw because they do not want to get involved. The people leave or the pastor leaves. No one wins. The church dies and the devil gets his way. The personal issues are not dealt with and continue along with the people wherever they go.

God's way of dealing with this type of situation is found in Matthew 18. Confront individuals involved privately and address the issue. If there is no resolve, bring several others who are spiritual leaders and address it again. If there is no resolve, bring it to the Church, and if the people do not listen to the Church remove, them until such time that they repent and turn from their ways to God's ways. (Matthew 18; 1st Corinthians 5) If they repent, they are to be forgiven and restored to fellowship like nothing ever happened. (2nd Corinthians 2:5-11)

The Lord had told me, "You will not be moved by man, but by My Spirit when it is My time." Again He gave me a Word. (Isaiah 41:9-16) The Word of the Lord will sustain you at all times in your life.

I took no delight when the Lord led these people out of the congregation. The Lord had enabled me to love them although they would not let me minister to them. This grieved my heart.

Yes, the Lord leads people in and He leads them out! Another time a person told me, "I believe the Lord is leading me out of this church," (meaning the person was off to a "better" place). I replied, "Yes, I believe the Lord is moving you on." (Unfortunately, in some cases wherever people were moving on to was not going to be a better place unless they repented.)

What people do not understand is that you take your bitterness, personal issues, and internal conflict with you. You cannot run away from issues. They need to be dealt with and removed.

Ministers need to work together as a team to help and care for God's people. Many is the time I have met people from other churches bad-mouthing the pastor where they had been previously. I had to tell them, "If you want to be a part of this ministry (I do not care how spiritual or wealthy they say they are), you will need to make things right with your previous pastor so you can come with a clean heart and report."

It is just a matter of care for the fellow minister, the people, and the Body of Christ.

We ministers can have issues as well. I have found it helpful to ask the Holy Spirit to examine my life, heart, and my mind to see if I am living displeasing to God, or if I am holding anything towards anyone that is not acceptable to God (or me as a minister of the Lord Jesus Christ). I want to know from the Holy Spirit the truth about me, known or unknown, that it may be revealed to me so I can change it by God's grace (Psalm 139:23-24) in Jesus' name. (See *Helping People* Book)

We do not have to demean and dishonor another brother or God's ministry through him to build up and promote ourselves and our own ministry. (Note: "My" ministry is not God's ministry) All that the Father has for each of us (God's team) to do (and care for) will come to us. (John 6:37-40) No selfish ambition, striving, competing or comparing (1st Corinthians 3:4-7), just faithfulness to the Lord, one's self, and others, building together the kingdom of God.

Jesus says, *"My sheep* (the ones entrusted to His care) *know my voice and they follow me."* (John 10:1-21) Not everyone is given to your care. Those who are will stay with you without your trying to hold on to them. They know where God has placed them.

Father, forgive me for the times that I have not been faithful to You, myself, and my brothers and sisters in Christ. In Jesus' name.

MINISTERS OF CHRIST IN UNITY

Ministers should have the same care for one another as they do for themselves. Matthew 18 applies to ministers as well as to the people of God. The care for fellow ministers should take as much (or more) precedent for the minister of God as the care of the people does.

If the ministers of Christ would come together in cities united in fellowship, prayer, and counsel, the ministry would be strong, the people equipped and mobilized, and everyone would be cared for. This is what we see in the book of Acts with the early church. They worked as one team, not many teams competing against and cautious with each other (The fruit of self-perpetuating man's organizations and belief divisions). The ministers would know each other, support each other, and work together in true fellowship, pleasing God. (Psalm 133)

I was trained to run campus student affairs at one of the largest seminaries in the world until church politics (man's selfish ambition, party spirit, power grab, or manipulation) and the "diversity" of belief and doctrine caused division in the denomination. It is a shame to us that the Church is one company with many divisions. Before Jesus returns it needs to become one church with no division. Jesus says, *"Any kingdom divided against itself will be ruined, and a house divided against itself will fall."* (Luke 11:17)

Along with others, Martin Luther took part in the Reformation. He would still have remained a monk if the church had not declared him a heretic, excommunicated him, and sought to kill him. His heart by the Holy Spirit was to clean up practices, like selling forgiveness and other beliefs of the church which were not of God. He wanted to bring the ministry (the priesthood of all believers) the Word of God so they too could read and understand God's Word, not dependant on Mary, the saints, the pope, or any man in order to go to God like Jesus had taught. (John 16:25-28) The Lord wanted to rule His church.

What the Lord started as a reformation from within the Church was thrown outside, rejected by the Church. It had become corrupted by the world's influences of power, wealth, and man's ambition for greatness. All who opposed it were to be removed and destroyed. (John 16:1-4)

Unfortunately opportunists, kings and others were quick to jump in for personal gain and saw this as an opportunity to break away from the papal rule and control. Man's politics began to corrupt what started as a pure movement of God (to reform His church and get it back on His course) into a political movement which later led to division (of belief) in the Church, which we still have today.

The same hierarchal organizational arrangement exists today in many of the churches side by side with the "free-lance"— the "I am doing my own thing" ministries. I have been in both camps. Neither one accepts anyone who is outside their group and cautions those who do.

Where is the team working? I believe only the Holy Spirit can bring this to pass. Even Peter, Paul, and Barnabas had to learn to work together and appreciate God working in and through the other. It takes desire and time together to make things happen. Is a visit with that minister as important as the visit with a parishioner who has money? I say, more important.

Some ministers have a genuine service, love and care for fellow ministers. Others do not realize the benefit of such association because it does not further their ministry. Others associate to advance their ministry. When they get what they want, they are gone. What about faithfulness to each other?

AN UNEXPECTED EXPERIENCE

I was thrust into the world of church politics which is like being thrown to the sharks. Who ministers to the minister? Like iron sharpens iron, brothers can sharpen each other. (Proverbs 27:17)

I thrust myself into it unknowingly. I had gone to the leaders of the church organization to seek guidance and to give a good report about what was happening in the church. What I would call a "check in and a check up." I went to gather with the rest of the team and had to leave alone.

In my thoughts ministry and spiritual things should have precedent over the political, but I was already judged and condemned. Because I would not take "sides" in the denominational spirit I was ostracized. I believe in doing what the Lord says, *"He who meddles in another man's strife takes a dog by the ears."* (Proverbs 26:17) The Lord told me that I had gone to Egypt (the world) and would have trouble.

I was just seeking to love the Lord and to love and care for His people the best I could in Jesus and to be part of the team. I quickly learned that organizations do not always have the best interest of their ministers at heart, but are in reality self-serving. Without my knowledge they had been listening to and meeting with the handful of people who were trying to control the church. Rather than speaking to me directly about the situation, they had been working against the ministry of the Lord, politicking with the same handful of people who had driven away five ministers before me.

Now I understood why I had received another call to a church on the coast. This church had ten times the members, three times the salary, and with a team of ministers where I would just do my field of expertise. I inquired of the Lord about it, and He told me, "Son, it is sucker bait!" I declined it.

Shortly thereafter, I received a letter and a phone call from the president of one of the largest insurance agencies in America, offering me a position with their company. Salary beyond my dreams, especially since I had just found out that Diana and I were eligible for welfare on the salary the church was paying me. (We were happy and blessed in spite of it. We were serving the Lord. What a privilege!) (1st Timothy 6:3-12)

I inquired of the Lord, and again He said, "Son, sucker bait." I declined the offer. My dad was a top club underwriter for one of the other largest insurance companies.

It was clear to me that officials from the denomination had spoken to these people to move me on to another situation. Follow your spirit and let the Lord direct your path, not men. (Proverbs 3:5-6) Be willing to accept the consequences of what such action may entail — persecution.

UNDERGOING PERSECUTION

Those who will be godly (led by the Lord's Spirit doing the will of God) will undergo persecution. The glory of the Lord will rest upon you and the Lord will lead you into what He has to complete your life and ministry. One's response to persecution will make or break you in the ministry. (See *Glory Crown* book and *Loving Witness* booklet) *"Many are the afflictions of the righteous, but the Lord delivers him out of them all."* (Psalm 34:19) (See Psalm 34 & 91)

The devil works through magnified reports of discontent and problems, seeking to create fear, troubles, and war. He wants to distract the minister and the people from doing the will of God (ministry) and praising the Lord (what we are created for). When persecution comes, refuse to get caught up in it or respond to it. Jesus shut his mouth. Keep your focus on the Lord and ministry. The Lord will be your defender. Love people and do good. The battle is not yours. Submit yourself to the Father who judges justly (1st Peter 2:18-23) and *"Resist* [take authority over] *the devil and he will flee from you."* (James 4:7)

People are not the enemy. They are being used and abused and will be cast aside and destroyed by the thief. Be there for them when that happens. (Read Romans 8, 12:9-21; Matthew 10; and 1st and 2nd Peter) *"Do not be overcome by evil, but overcome evil with good."* (Romans 12:21)

Jesus says, "Do not resist evil." Let evil burn itself out. Do not respond to the attacks by trying to defend yourself or the Lord. The Lord is your defender. He will defend His ministry and His ministers. Draw near to the Lord, obey Him and He will draw near to you. Praise the Lord and give Him thanks in all situations. (Romans 12:9-21)

Jesus says, "The world will hate you (John 15-16, Matthew 10) for His name's sake." At the point of persecution is where one's popularity with man ends and one's true obedience and life with God begins. If one seeks glory from man, compromise will happen which causes no glory from or for the Lord.

"Woe to you when all men speak well of you, for so did their fathers to the false prophets," Jesus says. (Luke 6:26) *"The fear of man brings a snare."* (Proverbs 29:25) *"I will never leave you nor forsake you. So we may boldly say: 'The Lord is my helper; I will not fear what man can do to me?' "* (Hebrews 13:5-6; Joshua 1:5-9)

When I looked for the approval and help of man by going to the denominational leaders, the Lord told me I had gone to the world. The Lord knew that these particular leaders were worldly and not as godly as I had thought. I was thinking that we were God's team, caring for the Lord's ministry, but they were about their purposes to preserve their organization and belief system.

Like Jesus was persecuted by the church of His upbringing, the council believed lies of a few people who wanted to control the church and attempted to remove me from the pastorate and ministry. (In man's church this can be done, but not in God's church.)

However, the Lord had told me, "You will not be moved by man, but by My Spirit." I am the Lord's minister, not called by man or by myself, but called and anointed by the Lord Jesus Christ to serve Him and His church.

A minister of the Lord must know to whom he must give an account. (1st Corinthians 4:1-5) A vote (man's church) was held at the church whether or not I would continue to be their pastor. All the people except for the few who wanted control of the church, voted for me to stay as their pastor.

"If God be for us who can be against [or condemn] *us."* (Romans 8:31:1) (Read Romans 8:31-39) Touch not God's anointed. (1st Chronicles 16:22) (Read Psalm 2, and Isaiah 54:14-17)

The Lord had run the meeting. It was a great victory for the kingdom and the people in God. False spirituality and tyranny were broken. I was not even at the meeting to answer the false charges. (2nd Timothy 1:12; 1st Peter 2:18-24) The Lord had me elsewhere at a conference where the Lord touched me and I released all my cares and the care of the congregation to Him. I forgave the people, for they really did not know what they were doing. (You do not oppose the Lord and His ministers, and think you can be blessed.)

IN THE LORD'S HANDS

I had the peace of God and angels ministered to me that night as I slept, attending to me (Matthew 4:11) and making sure I was alright. I awoke refreshed and went back home to find out what had happened at the meeting.

Whatever the case, I knew my life and my family were in the Lord's hands. (Jeremiah 29:11-14) I knew who I had believed and that His plans for us were for good, not for evil, to prosper us and to give us a hope and a future. It was not about me, but about God's kingdom advancing. (Philippians 1:12-30)

The Lord had also put with us then and to this day faithful people who love the Lord and us, encouraging us and helping us fulfill what the Lord has called us to do. We thank the Lord for each one of them —

past, present, and future. *Bless them always, Father, and give to them all that you have for them spiritually, mentally, physically, financially, and in relationships.* And they have been blessed (2nd Chronicles 20:20) over the years.

Those who have opposed the work of the Lord and His ministers have not fared as well. Although we as God's ministers must lovingly bless, forgive, and do good to those who oppose us, the Lord will deal with them. Unless they repent and turn from opposing the Lord and His ministers, they will receive what they have sown. God is not mocked. (Galatians 6:7-10; Romans 12:17-21)

It has not been a time of rejoicing for me to see the awful things that happen to people that oppose the Lord and His servants. What is even worse is that many of them were destroyed because they, like Satan, would not humble themselves and seek God's forgiveness and help.

Like Miriam, Korah, and Pharaoh who opposed Moses, many others have brought tragedy upon themselves by thinking more highly of themselves and opposing the Lord and His servants. I have seen cancers, blindness, loss of job, family, sanity, and death come upon such people.

One in particular during this time bothered me. After the Lord and the people had chosen me to stay as pastor, he came to me, "Pastor, what do I need to do to make it right with the Lord and you? (He had been used [fool working] by the scorners to work against the ministry.) I told him, "You need to ask the Lord, myself, Diana, and the congregation for forgiveness… and tell them the truth."

In my presence he asked the Lord's forgiveness and my forgiveness. That week he asked Diana's forgiveness. On Sunday he was supposed to ask the congregation's forgiveness. We were so excited for him, but he did not come to church. My heart sank. (Apparently, he had let the other people talk him out of doing this. Naturally!) Monday he had a massive heart attack and died instantly. I grieved. It was such a needless loss. (Years later his son went into the ministry because of the Lord's influence through us.)

LEARNING HOW TO LOVE

Ministers of God remember this: *"Whoever turns a sinner from the way of error will save them from death and cover over a multitude of sins."* (James 5:20) (See also Galatians 6:1-5, Jude 1:20-23) We are to save, not to call down the fire. (Luke 9:54-55) "Bless, do not curse!" the Lord kept telling me.

I have also seen many more come back to God and to us to receive deliverance from the Lord, like when Job prayed for his friends. Jesus prayed for us, "Father, forgive them," which enabled us to be saved.

"If your enemy hungers, feed him. If he is thirsty, give him something to drink" (Romans 12:20). *"Do not be overcome by evil, but overcome evil with good."* (Romans 12:21) (See Romans 12:17-21) You really learn how to love when you have opposition. You really learn about your own heart when you go through persecution.

"Humble yourselves under the mighty hand of God, that He may exalt you in due time, casting all your cares upon Him, for He cares for you." (1st Peter 5:6-7) (See also 2:1-11)

"When a man's ways please the Lord, He makes even his enemies to be at peace with him." (Proverbs 16:7) When the sacrificial love and peace of God is in your heart towards those who are opposing Jesus in you, not you, then you are growing in maturity in Christ. (Matthew 10:5-42; Romans 12:9-21)

It is God's loving kindness (Romans 2:4) through us that enables those who oppose themselves to get free. We must not be quarrelsome but gentle, patient, ready to share and be there for them when the Lord opens the opportunity. (2nd Timothy 2:24-26) Am I willing to lay down my life for the Lord and the care of His people or not? (John 10:7-18)

Although I have experienced persecution in the later years of the ministry, it was this early experience that set the love of God and the people in my heart to prepare for the ministry. What the thief intended for evil to break me and remove me from the ministry, through persecution, God intended for good as His glory and grace grew in me, empowering me to be His man and to become a shepherd after His heart, caring for His people. (See *Loving Witness* booklet) (Read 2nd Peter; 2nd Corinthians 12:9) (See *The Kindness Factor* and *God's Loving Kindness* books)

It was all about commitment to the Lord, commitment to myself to be a godly man, and His working in me and other people (my wife, my family, and the people in the ministry). As I look back at this three year period, I see the Lord had given me a "baptism of fire" course in Holy Spirit ministry. The Lord was preparing me for what was to come. Nothing was more important to me than knowing Christ Jesus my Lord, the power of His resurrection, and the fellowship of sharing in His sufferings, becoming like him in His death, and so attaining the resurrection from the dead. (Read Philippians 3)

OPPRESSION WAS LIFTED

The Lord gives seasons of "refreshing in the Holy Spirit." (Acts 3:19-20) These are growth and revelation times in our lives when our walk with God is deepened and strengthened. I had come again to such a point. The Lord had brought a time of peace.

He had said, "You will not be moved by man, but by My Spirit." People and devils do not control your life. We who are sons of God are led by the Spirit of God. (Romans 8:14; Matthew 10; Joshua 1:5-9) Jesus laid down His life for our salvation. His life was not taken from Him. No one could touch him until it was His time by the Father in heaven. (John 10:18)

When the people who were divisive went to another church, the congregation flourished. The oppression had lifted for us. I had always thought it interesting that the ministers did not cooperate together to hold people accountable for their actions and so care for the Body of Christ, like Jesus and Paul did. (1st Corinthians 5; Romans 16:17-20; Matthew 18:15-18)

What I learned was that man's ministry is not about the advancement and building up of the Body of Christ (the Church) and the kingdom of God. It is not about caring for God's ministers and people in God's way according to the Word of God. Rather, man's church in contrast to God's church is concerned about money, politics, how many people are in the church (numbers), reputation, and show. Sin is not dealt with, but condoned.

The Lord is more concerned about His Church being holy and pure than He is about it being full. Throughout history problems have arisen because ministers and people have not taught and submitted to God's Word and standard for life and living. Without holiness no one is going to see the Lord. (Hebrews 12:14-29)

"You will know them by their fruit," Jesus says. (Matthew 7:13-23) *"Have nothing to do with those who have a form of godliness, but deny the power of godliness."* (Read 2nd Timothy 3-4:8; 2nd Peter 2; 1st John 2:15-17, 28-3:10; 1st Timothy 6:3-5; and Jude)

TESTIFY TO THE GLORY OF GOD

During this time two impressions had come to me. One was of Moses before Pharaoh — "Let my people go." The second was of Jesus before Pilate. The Lord gave me understanding about what was happening and what would happen. Like Paul knew in the Spirit that he must go to Jerusalem and on to Rome, I knew that I must go to the higher boards of the church. Then the Lord would direct me into what He wanted accomplished to His glory and purpose. In their evaluation, they found no fault in person or ministry and integrity in my life.

The Lord wanted me to testify about what He was doing for His glory. The earlier boards were accusatory yet had no evidence of fault, like Jesus before Caiaphas. The higher board consisted of spiritual men who were seeking the Lord.

One of the men kept speaking to the chief administrator, "What are the charges against this man? We find no fault with him." He was part of the legal counsel. The chief administrator was silent. His aide apologized for his part in listening to and acting upon the disgruntled people's lies in seeking to remove me. They then wanted me to respond as to what this was all about.

It was time to testify to the glory of God. (Mathew 10:12-28) This was not about my life and ministry. As Paul said, "This has all happened for the furtherance of God's gospel." (Philippians 1:12)

The thief, the "accuser of the brethren," will attempt to get you to defend and focus on yourself, but remember this is not about you — the Lord is positioning you to testify to His glory. What is intended for evil the Lord is going to turn to good for His glory to accomplish His purpose. (Gen 50:20) Stay focused on Him.

As I testified to the glory of God (His presence) and all the wonderful things He was doing, there was not a dry eye in the place. A great thankfulness was present for who the Lord is and what He does. It is in such an environment that the Lord speaks and acts.

When I concluded, a man of God who had pastored for forty years spoke to me saying, "Pastor, there is no question that the Lord has called you to great things in His service. Unfortunately, there is no provision for such a ministry in the denomination."

He was apologizing for the denomination, and I was listening to what the Lord was directing me to do through him.

Next, looking across the room I saw the glory of God on the man who kept saying, "What are the charges against this man?" I knew the Lord was going to speak again. He said, "You cannot change the system." (I did not know that I was attempting to change the system. I was just seeking to love God, care for His people, and do what God's Word says.) He continued, "If Luther could not change the system, neither can you. Here are your choices: conform to the system, leave the system, or stay and have problems."

WE MUST OBEY GOD

The Lord had spoken to me. I have never believed that the Lord wants rebellion in people's hearts. I honor the authorities of God in my life. They have helped me to make the life-direction decision the Lord wanted me to make.

The minister of God must obey God's system rather than man's system. If man's system rejects you because of God's system, praise God! Do not get hurt or bitter, finding fault, but trust the Lord for what He has for you and move on. The early church would have stayed in Jerusalem if they had not gotten persecuted.

We prayed that the will of the Lord be done. I chose to move on to what the Lord would have me to do. They gave me ministerial letters of recommendation with doctrinal differences.

The Lord had told me that "I would not be moved by man but by His Spirit." It was the time to move — into the next phase of life and ministry.

Upon returning home I called for a congregational meeting. It is important to the Lord to bring closure and reconciliation. Although I could have taken the buildings, people, and started a new ministry, I believed they were not mine to take. They were the Lord's, as He had expressed to me, "They are My sheep." This was in response to my concern for the care of the people.

The Lord said, "They are My sheep, and I will take care of them. You go do what I have given you to do!"

Knowing that the Lord would take care of the people, I was comforted. I knew my charge and responsibility for their care was to be passed on to another. I was free to move on — business finished, task accomplished. Like Jesus at the cross, "It is finished."

In the will, power, and authority of the Holy Spirit, the Lord addressed the people for the last time through me. I opened the Bible to 1st Corinthians 13 and read it to them. The Lord moved on their hearts as I released them to the Lord's care. One of the people who would not respond to God's loving ministry because he wanted to control the congregation broke down in tears receiving God's love, forgiveness, and reconciliation (God's love never fails). He stood up and recommended to the people that they send me and my family off with blessing and monetary provision. (Just like the Lord supplied when the Israelites left Egypt.)

Diana, my daughter Erin, and I began our new adventure in the Holy Spirit, the work of faith — not knowing what was to become, but trusting the Lord to be with us and order our steps. (Proverbs 3:5-6) My parents thought I had gone crazy by leaving the "faith of the family." (Matthew 10:32-42 — Jesus' family)

At that time, they did not understand, as they do now, that it is not about what church you go to, but rather it is about your relationship to Jesus

Christ and the Word of God through the Holy Spirit. There is only one true church of the Lord Jesus Christ. (Ephesians 2:11-22, 4:1-16) All divisions are caused by man's unbelief, ignorance, and traditions.

A Servant Of CHRIST

PART 2

NEW BEGINNINGS

During the next year Diana and I, having left everything, grew together and learned a new appreciation for the Lord's presence, wisdom, guidance, and provision. Like the children of Israel, the Lord was leading us to the next phase of life and ministry that He had daily prepared for us. (Deuteronomy 8, Joshua 1:5-9, Proverbs 3:5-6)

As in all wilderness experiences (Israel, Jesus, Paul, etc.), we drew near to the Lord, trusting and relying on Him. He proved Himself faithful. The Lord knew what plans He had and how to carry out His plans. (Jeremiah 29:11-12) We did not, so we had to wait on the Lord and trust Him to reveal what He wanted and how He wanted to do it. (James 1:5-8)

"Without a vision My people perish," the Lord says. For everything the Lord does He supplies a vision (purpose), a plan (how to accomplish His vision), the personnel He wants involved, provision (supplies) to accomplish the vision, and policies in how to operate the vision.

The Lord never does isolated events. Everything He does has a purpose which will bring Him glory and effects many lives through the testimonies of what He has done in you and through you. (Zephaniah 3:8)

<u>GUIDELINES FOR NEW BEGINNINGS:</u>

1. Forget the past — press ahead to the future. (Philippians 3:14-16)
2. Jesus learned obedience through the things He suffered. (Hebrews 5:7-10) Persecution builds character and purifies motive.

3. Have no independence, rebellion (1st Peter 2:13-24) or unforgiveness in your heart. Such attitudes will make you and your message impure now and for the future.
4. Do what you know to do (love people, preach the Word, do good, destroy the work of the devil) (Acts 10:38) until you get specific vision, direction, and wisdom from the Lord.
5. Trust the Lord moment by moment. Do not try to make something happen to save and secure self. (Luke 12:22-53) Praise and acknowledge the Lord and He will direct the path. (Proverbs 3:5-6, Joshua 1:5-9, Matthew 10)
6. Be willing to be alone with God until He links you with others who will share in the vision with you.
7. Seek the Lord and His wisdom. (James 1:2-8)
8. Be patient. Spend time in the Word, prayer, and fasting.
9. Listen and obey the Lord's direction when it comes.
10. Beware of counterfeit visions and directions. You must do what the Lord has given to you in your heart and not another's desire. (Matthew 16:21-23, Acts 21:12-14, directed by God, not man Genesis 16).

In our lifetimes there are various growth or new beginning times which effect or create trauma — spiritually, mentally, physically, financially, and in our relationships. It is very important that during these transition times we draw near and wait upon the Lord to hear His direction and vision. Such action will keep us in balance until we receive our vision and instruction — the appointing and anointing to fulfill the Lord's plan and purpose.

The Lord will then also give to us the proper plan to carry out the vision, people, policies, and provision.

We cannot afford to allow pressures from within (spiritual and mental) and without us (family, finances, etc.) to distract or hinder us from God's plan.

The Lord taught me "Sure (based on His principles and promise), Slow (no hasty decisions—time is our friend), Steady (keep going — press ahead go with what you know) Steps (faith and obedience steps) equal Success (God's will and purpose accomplished).

During the following year, as I was waiting on the Lord for His vision, I began to write books (*The Love Disciple* and *Victory*) and to hold house group meetings.

The Lord then moved us to a laundromat to hold services. He was sorting out and choosing who was to be with us. Only a true believer and seeker would bring their own chair and come to worship God in a laundromat. We saw miracles. As one 89 year old woman stated, "Pastor, this is so wonderful. Where else could we go to wash our clothes and wash our sins away?" Others who wanted to know where we were holding services, never showed up when they found out it was a laundromat (and you had to bring a chair).

Our shortest service was in this place — five minutes. As I recall, the Lord said to me, "I'm leaving. Tell the people to come back when they are ready to worship Me." I did, and the next week they were early and ready.

We were learning to be led by the Holy Spirit during those years, not that you ever stop learning. Years later I had a thought to try to make the service an hour long, only to have it end up lasting over five hours. It was like Balaam attempting to curse Israel. Every time he opened his mouth he blessed Israel. *"What God has blessed cannot be cursed."*

It is the Lord's service. He will have His way and we allow Him to do what He wants to His glory and our good. Since 1978, I have seen services or messages similar but not the same. Ask the Lord what He wants to do and teach and how He wants to do it.

Finding a quiet place to hear the Lord is so important. One day as I was listening for the Lord He began to give to me the assignment and the vision details which I had been waiting for. (See *Vision* book)

THE VISION

1. That He would call up supportive laborers. Some would be givers, some would be prayers, and some would go out and work with us. These people would come from all over the place, and God would sort out who would be with us and who would not.
2. We would be "a servant to the servants." As He put it, "a minister to the ministers." He was showing me how many of God's ministries and ministers do not really have anybody to encourage them, so that is what He was calling us up to do. We were to work with equipping people for the work of the ministry and work with people who are already in ministry. We were to encourage, correct, motivate, and work with people coming up in the Body, and we were to help them grow to take the place that God had for them.
3. Even before the word was given, God was doing just that. He was sending us ministers and people who were in ministry or coming up in the ranks who were later going to be ministering. Many of them are now ministering, but God gave them what they needed at that time. Teaching ministers to minister in a "school of the prophets'" is also part of the vision.

   We are to minister to the entire body of Christ, not just certain segments in the world. Rather, we are to encourage and motivate believers and enable groups and people to have the fullness of the Spirit to teach and to work. Thus we work with all denominations. We work with all God's people wherever they may be. We share the love of God and the fullness of the Spirit with them, teaching people to move in the gifts of the Spirit and the fullness of God's operation. We teach them to lift up Jesus, not individual groups, and not to promote individuals, groups, or particular denominations or non-denominations. As Jesus has promised, He will draw all men unto Himself.

The Lord ministered to me that, similar to the relationship between Jesus and the disciples, I was to pastor those whom God sent to work with us. However, like Jesus, the ministry is to the Body beyond a local setting. Jesus was not called to pastor the multitudes. He operated in a prophet's office ministering to the multitudes.

4. We are able to be like a hospital. As God moves in power in the ministry, He sets people free. We see people healed and delivered spiritually, mentally, emotionally, physically, and delivered from the power of Satan. Just like in the bible, the demons come out. This is why the Spirit of the Lord is upon us to mend the broken-hearted, to heal marriages, to draw people to the Lord, and to heal their minds and bodies. (Luke 4:18, 19) God put the anointing upon us to do that work. He showed that we would be a hospital in the ministry and that sick people (whether spiritually, mentally, emotionally, or physically) would be coming. They would be coming from all over (as they are doing now). God, by His power, is setting the people free to rejoice in Him. All the Father has for us will come to us. (John 6)

   He said that there are also many healthy people in a hospital who do various functions so that the hospital might operate properly. We are praising God that the workers are increasing so that more work can be accomplished.

5. The Lord said that many people would not understand, but He would give the increase. He said we would lift up Jesus and sow the word of God through all the medias. Several years after that word was given, the radio ministry had expanded internationally. International television, books, newspaper columns, tapes, internet, and every form of media that we know of were happening and are now expanding. These things are all happening to God's glory as He promised in His word.

6. Several years after the first word was given, the Lord spoke again, telling us that we would be a part of a major move of His Spirit in the last days, in leading His people into true worship. *The Everlasting Gospel* book came as a result of that word.
7. There is discipline involved in a vision:
   a.) We are not to rely on people or look to people for praise or criticism.
   b.) We are not ever to solicit any funds, which we never do. We are to look to God as our source. He places it on people's hearts to give, and they ask us what our needs are.
   c.) We are to seek glory from God, not from people. He said that our lives are no longer our own and that it is a responsibility to be faithful in proclaiming the word and in the use of God's gifts. Everything was to be done to His glory.

In 1978, when we asked the Lord for a name, what we were to call this work, the Lord told us, "You shall call it 'Glory to God Ministries,' for the work I will do shall bring glory to My name."

We of Glory to God Ministries desire to simply be faithful to God to do what He has given us to do to His glory in His body. We thank the Lord for His faithful support through you, encouraging us through your prayers, time, and giving for the furtherance of God's word.

The Lord began to send the faithful people who would pray, believing God, and givers, administrators, praisers, encouragers, and helps ministry workers. The work began to take form. Under the Lord's guidance, He began to show things before they would happen. He told me to "Thank Me for all the people that I send to you past — present — future."

All that the Father has for you will come to you. (John 6:37) I knew that whatever we would need would come to us when it was needed (proper vision, plans, policies, personnel, and provision).

On one occasion, He showed me a facility where He was planting a church. Since we were looking for a larger facility, I thought it was for us. Asking the owner, I was promptly informed that the place was not for sale or rent.

Two months later my friend's ministry moved in. I was learning that just because the Lord was showing me what was going to happen it did not mean necessarily it was for us. He was simply showing His will and purpose for His kingdom work.

All His ministries would always have a place to worship that He had prepared and would never lack for anything that is needed to do what the Lord has called each of His ministries to do as they trust and obey Him.

People who the Lord had prepared and sent to us were receiving wisdom and knowledge, healing and deliverance, restoration, and renewal. Miracles were regularly occurring. Ministers were being encouraged, refreshed, equipped, and empowered.

As the Lord had said, "Sow the Word to the nations through all the media," He began to order the doors to be opened. First, by giving books to be written, secondly, services provided tapes. Thirdly, He directed me to a local radio station which produced and aired the radio program for many years which provided radio tapes.

Under the Holy Spirit's direction the Lord ordered radio broadcasting around the world by directing what regions, cities and stations He wanted us to air on when He wanted us to air. We were not to solicit funds over the air, but to present the Word of God and the ministry of the Holy Spirit to the people.

Various broadcast agents would approach us, but we would seek the Lord's direction for the people we would work with and partner with. The Lord was very clear that He is our source and agent. Their heart must be like our heart and vision to advance God's kingdom and not promoting self or money.

I asked an agent who had solicited us about being on the radio (not knowing that we were on over 40 major U.S cities and overseas). "Why do you think that we should be on radio?" He gave me the reasons about expanding the ministry outreach, having a message to share that needs to be heard, etc.

I asked him another question. "Have you asked the Lord about whether or not we should be on the radio? If you really care about me and the ministry, you would ask this question. Otherwise, you are not doing me or any other minister a service. If God wants us on the air He will make a way and will pay for the air time. If God does not want us on the radio, you make your commission and we are in debt." He had no response and later called and thanked me for God's correction to his motivation.

Vanity and personal gain cannot be the motivation for a minister of God. It is a matter of faithfulness and obedience to the Lord. Someday we must give an account. What does the Lord want me doing and how does He want me to do it? *"A man's ways appear right to a man, but God searches the motivation of the heart."* (Proverbs 16:2) This is important to me.

A secular station manager with whom we had long term relationship asked me, "What should I do with this minister's program that is six months behind in payment?" I told him "a good rule is one month, a warning. Two months, off the air." This ministry should have been taken off the air long before then.

This was a major worldwide ministry which solicited funds throughout the program. Today they are bankrupt.

If you are going off the air because you do not get that person's ten dollars, maybe God does not want you on the radio or TV. One should evaluate in prayer the extent and purpose of the programming.

The Lord gets no glory from our bad debt. Again, the Lord pays for what He wants. By God's grace and management we have been broadcasting radio and TV since 1978 and have had no bad debt, without solicitation. The Lord taught me that "Thankful people give to the work of the Lord by the Lord's encouragement."

I believe the Lord tests our faith and motivation at times. Are we willing to let go of something that the Lord has given or given to do? (For instance, Abraham and Isaac). I remember a time when for about a year I kept approaching the Lord that I was willing to let go of the broadcasting if He wished. He told me that it was not yet the time. (Personally I do not have personal interest in anything I do. I am a servant just doing what I am directed to do. I am on God's assignment and must do and finish His will).

A year later, the Lord directed that it was time to stop broadcasting and allocate the funds in another direction. We stopped all broadcasting. Two years later He said it was time to broadcast again. The next day we were contacted by one of our previous satellite networks to air again. We began broadcasting as He directed.

THE STRATEGY

Lord, give to me the hearing ear and the instructed tongue that I might hear your direction and speak your Word when and where you want it spoken. (Isaiah 50:4) *"Trust the Lord lean not to your own understanding. Acknowledge Him in all your ways and He will direct your path."* (Proverbs 3:5-6)

Another time He had me just read the Word, not pray. Later I was just to pray for three months. Another time I was to meditate on Numbers 23:19 for 60 days and again for 90 days. He wanted me to know who He is and that "it is impossible that what man considers impossible to not happen when you act on My Word."

I asked the Lord why so many negatives. He said, "Because people are negative. All things are possible when you act on (obey) My Word!"

As a child I had learned to love and obey His Word. Now the Lord was teaching and instructing me to obey His voice (Spirit). The two will always agree. *"Those who are the sons of God will be led and controlled by the Spirit of God."* (Romans 8:14)

The Lord taught me to "never launch two rockets at once." I was not to start two programs at the same time. We could be developing, planning, etc., but not to launch two things at once. Hence, once the services, books, and radio were operating, then the Lord began the TV development and launch.

It is interesting that when you are serving God and man, ministry doors are opened by the Lord. As Jesus said, *"He who shall be called great in the kingdom...* (Matthew 5:19) *must become ...the servant of all.*" (Mark 9:35) God's heart is with people. As He told me, "Love My people. Care for My people. For I am coming soon."

THE MESSAGE

The message we share is God's love message — the gospel. Repent (turn from your own life), believe on the Lord Jesus (God's life will come to you), and become saved and sanctified (become one with God and His family). Bring heaven to people, not hell. Advance the kingdom of God.

- The Lord loves you with an everlasting love (Jeremiah 31:3)
- He will never leave or forsake you so you can boldly say the Lord is my helper I will not fear what man shall do to me (Hebrews 13:5-6)
- The Lord's plans for you are for good, not evil — to prosper you and to give you hope and a future (Jeremiah 29:11-12)

- You are created to be to the praise of God's glory (Ephesians 1). He wants you to work with Him to bring heaven to the people.

> Key ministry scriptures: Proverbs 3:5-6, Philippians 4:4-19, Joshua 1:5-9, Luke 4:18-19, and Luke 10:18-20, Isaiah 61, Mark 11:22-25, Genesis 50:20.

"How God anointed Jesus of Nazareth with the Holy Spirit and power. He went around doing good (the will of God), *healing all who were oppressed of the devil, for God was with him."* (Acts 10:38)

"To them that believe the works that I do, you will do and greater works will you do because I go to the Father. Whatever you ask in my name I will do that the Father be glorified in the Son." (John 14:12-13)

One day I received a call from Portland, Oregon. As I was speaking with the man, the Lord directed me to get on the plane and to be a "stabilizer" to him.

Over the years, I have found that the Lord has sent me to a city for one person and then did many other things as a result of that divine appointment.

For three days I went with the man. The first day we visited the hospital where his dad was not given a week to live. We prayed over his heart and left to work with the man's personal affairs. His wife had left him taking the children. He had lost his job. He was suicidal. Everything in his life was coming to an end, but God had other plans.

We contacted his wife and I ministered to her God's Word and Spirit seeking to stabilize their situation. She was relieved that he was getting help and she was constrained from doing anything rash and diffused of bitterness.

The next day, we received a call from the hospital that his dad was being released. They had run more tests and they could find nothing wrong with his heart. The Lord had healed him. (He lived for another ten years.) We picked him up and continued to share the Lord's goodness, building on hope, faith, and the future.

The third day he drove me to a TV studio. As I sat in the lobby, the Lord gave me the thought that I would minister to everyone in the studio that day. He met me in the lobby with the owner and president of the studio and a Christian TV network.

I was asked to be on the president's program that day. The peace of God fell upon the place as the Lord had given me to minister God's peace to the people. When the interview finished, I was asked to pray in a separate room for the staff. Just like the Lord has said.

Following the prayer time, one of the staff walked over to me and told me that the Lord had told him that I "needed" a microwave. This person had no knowledge of a discussion Diana and I had about a microwave. I had told her that we did not "need" a microwave. Apparently, the Lord thought differently. I received the microwave when I returned home. God is good! (I used it the most.)

Before leaving, the president of the network spoke to me, inviting me to return and do a 13 week pilot program. I did. This led to three more 13 week programs giving us one full year of TV programming. These tapes were then presented to other stations and the TV ministry began.

Later, we approached a local station which we aired on for TV production of more tapes. This led to the person who was producing our programs having an encounter with the Holy Spirit as the Lord revealed his life (like the woman in John 4). He became part of the ministry. As the Lord blessed his life, he became a blessing to the ministry. Years later he became our TV and audio producer as the Lord supplied for our own production studio.

Sure-slow-steady-steps = God's success (His will and purpose accomplished)

Time is our friend. Be patient and believe God! The Lord makes all things beautiful in its time. (Ecclesiastes 3:11) There is a time for everything under heaven. (Ecclesiastes 3:1) Seek first the kingdom of God (Be about God's business loving His people). He supplies and takes care of everything that is needed for the life and ministry He has called you to do. You do not build the ministry, God does. *"Except the Lord build the house your labor is in vain..."* (Psalm 127)

Three months later the man, who needed to be stabilized, became a stabilizer. His family was restored, his Dad was healed. He started a new enterprise to God's glory. What was intended for evil, the Lord turned to His glory and the good of (only God knows how many) lives worldwide, which has resulted through the sowing of God's Word through the media.

The Lord told me, "Son, you will never know all the lives that I have touched through My ministry. We will reach the world one person at a time. The world is small. (I saw the world as a very small drop in His hand. The next day satellite TV opened up to us.) Just be faithful to do your part which I have given to you. No more and no less. Be encouraged, your labor is not in vain. (Joshua 1:6-9)

The Lord said, "I am with you to help you to finish and receive all that I have prepared for you." He told me not to pray that people live or die, but that they come into and finish all that He has given them to do. I have had many opportunities to depart this life and to be in paradise with the Lord, which is my desire, but the Lord keeps sending me back to help the people to finish what He has given me to do. (See *Safe Place* and *Patience* books)

HUMBLE BEGINNINGS

"Your beginnings will seem humble, so prosperous will be your future." (Job 8:7) The Lord told me to always remember the humble beginnings when He is your trust, source, and everything. As the years go by and the Lord does what He says He will do (Numbers 23:19) it is easy to forget from whence you came. Greatness is determined by faithfulness to the Lord, not by accomplishment. When we stand before the Lord all we want to hear Him say is, "Well done, faithful child! Come and receive all My pleasures that I have prepared for you!" (See Deuteronomy 8)

COVERING

Having been moved by the Lord from the denomination that I was raised in, I felt the Lord wanted me under a "covering" or authority. The Lord's early church had an order as a functioning body of ministers and ministries working together under the Lord's authority, unlike today where men dictate by forming organizations around belief systems, policies, and operations.

If the Lord moves you to His original biblical working, where do you fit in? The Body of Christ today is so fragmented and divided by belief that we need to get back to what the Lord says (belief) and function (operation).

In my experience I found that the Lord did not want me to "join" another denomination or "covering," but rather to function in the Body of Christ as Moses, Isaiah, Elijah, Paul, Peter, Timothy, etc. The Lord is the "covering" for His church. Jesus is the Head. All other ministers and ministries are under His direction and cooperate one with another in the building and advance of the Lord's Kingdom and one church. (Read 1st Corinthians 3-4, and Ephesians 4).

As Paul had hands laid on him to be sent out and begin his missionary journeys, the Lord wanted me to "be sent out." He gave me the people He wanted to lay hands, and I was sent out to do what the Lord had given me to do in His one church. Ministries of the Lord Jesus are not independent or rebellious, but one with each other about the Father's business. Together we will see the goodness of the Lord in His church. We need to get to know each other and work together.

TIMES OF FAVOR AND REFRESHING

In the many years to follow the Lord's favor and refreshing caused His growth and expansion to occur. The Lord would reveal what He wanted before it happened. We were learning "to trust the Lord, lean not to our own understanding, and acknowledge Him in all our ways." (Proverbs 3:5-6) The Holy Spirit wants to lead and guide us. We need to learn to hear and obey His voice.

The Lord said, "Sure (based on His principles and promises), Slow (time is our friend; do nothing in haste), Steady (stay with it, keep going) Steps (be obedient to action on direction given) = God's Success (will and purpose accomplished).

ESTABLISH A BASE

The Word of the Lord (direction of the Holy Spirit) had become exceedingly important to my heart. It gave inspiration, vision, direction, correction, comfort, encouragement, and guidance (warning and instruction). We must seek the Lord where He wants us to be and what He wants us to do and then be obedient.

One day He said, "Go to the desert. I want you to be a part of a major move of My Spirit in that region." On another day, He said, "The whole world goes to that area. Establish a base (headquarters) from which we will take My Word to the nations of the world." The headquarters became known as "the city of habitation," based on the Word in Psalm 107.

The Lord would bring the people who needed to receive from the Lord to us or He would bring the Word which was going to the nations to them. The Lord said, "We will reach the world — one person at a time."

Everything is by divine appointment. In many cases when all else has failed, the Lord sends us people who are at the worst or lowest moment in their lives, and the Lord works His miracles.

He told me, "I can put Humpty Dumpty together again." (Referring to the nursery tale about an egg sitting on a wall — had a great fall and nothing could put him together again.) The Lord says and does put lives back together and better and wiser than before if people continue in His Word.

THE CITY OF HABITATION

More than a place of buildings, the city of habitation is an environment in which the Holy Spirit is free to move and create newness and refreshing in people's lives. A touch of heaven and God's glory, which creates God's new creation as people continue in His Word, they will experience heaven on earth. As Jesus said, *"The kingdom of heaven is within you"* — who can build a house for the Lord? But the Lord has placed His Spirit within us. His glory will fill us and everything around us.

TRUST & OBEY — GOD'S PROVISION

Over the next thirty years, the Lord began a series of obedience adventures involving land acquisitions. He had told us that we would always have a place to worship. Each time He directed us to purchase a property we thought this was where He wanted us to build, but He had other plans as it unfolded. This was actually how He financed His ministry and outreach over the years and paid for the existing facilities we are using.

When the Lord does something, He does not just do one thing; He does many things and has many purposes for what He does. Some are revealed immediately, and others are for long term. This is why it is so difficult for man to discern and understand the infinite wisdom of the Lord. This is why the Lord says, *"Trust the Lord. Lean not to your own understanding, acknowledge Him in all your ways, and He will direct the path."* (Proverbs 3:5-6) *"The steps of the righteous are ordered of the Lord. Though he stumble he will not be utterly cast down."* (Read Psalm 37)

What people do not understand is that the Lord's ways are not man's ways nor man's ways the Lord's ways. Our part is to hear and obey the Lord, nothing more or less. He does not ask us what we think or whether we approve of His plan and ways. He does not have to ask us. He is the Lord. We are His servants. He receives the glory for what He does, not us. We receive the benefit.

It is not that we are so smart or so righteous. (Read Deuteronomy 8-9) The Lord does not reveal the whole plan. He just gives us our daily faith steps. It is easy to say when it is all done, "Look at what I did, and I knew that all the time." In reality, it was the Lord God who gave everything (power) to accomplish what He desired to His glory, not ours. (See Deuteronomy 8:16-19)

When all is said and done, we say, "We just did what the Lord directed us to do." He brought it to fruition and completion. It is His kingdom, glory, and power. He gives us the privilege to participate with Him in all that He is and has in Jesus Christ.

FAITH STRETCHERS & TESTS

The first property the Lord directed us to purchase required seventy-two thousand as a down payment. We had three days to proceed. I asked the Lord, "How are we going to do this?" He said, "Call for an offering." (I thought, *we don't have any services between now and then to call for an offering.*) "Take the plans and go talk to the owner." I obeyed, and the owner welcomed me. Before I had a chance to say anything the owner asked me about what was in my hand. I told him the plans of our vision. He proceeded to talk to me like it was his vision for over an hour about what we could do with the property.

After he was finished, he looked at me in a distinct (God) way and said, "Now, what was it you wanted to see me about?" I started to mention about the three days (I was going to tell him that we did not have the money), but he interrupted me and said, "I'll give you three months."

The Lord works His plan through everyone concerned. Always remember a good God deal blesses the buyer and the seller.

Most people would not have a problem with the next part about "call for an offering." However for seven years we had operated by the Lord's direction of teaching about the tithe and offering, a box out for offerings and not asking for money — just say, "Thankful people give to the work of the Lord." The Lord showed me Moses and the Tabernacle, and David and the Temple.

You cannot allow yourself to think that because the Lord does things in a certain way; He will not do it differently. Moses was told to stretch forth the staff, and then speak to the rock, but Moses struck it.

It is all about obedience and not allowing yourself to get in the way of God's purpose and plan. The people loved and responded to the Lord's call for an offering as they always have because they are thankful to him! (On the day before the seventy-two thousand was due, the last five thousand check was brought.)

The test in this was earlier when the call was given for the offering, Diana and I, with the people, asked the Lord what He wanted us to do. I heard clearly, "Give it all, last." I said, "Lord, you will have to show Diana this." Several days later, I came home and she looked at me saying, "I know what the Lord told you. He said, 'Give it all.' " She agreed to do it if she could write the check.

Another person (who could have paid the whole thing) approached me during the time of the offering and said that he would be willing to pay whatever the difference was if we were short at the end.

Do not lean to your own understanding or expectations about people either. Prejudice, partiality, favoritism are of the world and not of God. People are not always what they appear or make themselves out to be. We have had many people come to the ministry presenting their desire to bless the ministry with this or that, only to see their desire unfulfilled because they did not follow through and continue because their flesh gets in the way. (Proverbs 16:2, 18)

Let people prove themselves over time before you engage them in the work. Jesus said, "You will know them by their fruit and life." (Matthew 7) Do they put their time, talents, and treasures where there mouth is or not? *"Many profess unfailing love, but a faithful servant who can find?"*

All the down payment had been received. It was time for the test. Would we give all of our offering, some, or none? (Remember Ananias and Sapphira [Acts 5]) Of course! Diana and I would give all of everything in our life savings the way the Lord had directed both of us!

"To obey is better than sacrifice!" (1st Samuel 15:22-23) We were rejoicing with the Lord and the people. A few weeks later a group of

people (who did not know what we had done) came to us and gave us an all-inclusive trip to Hawaii. The Lord is good in His plans. Diana had always wanted to go to Hawaii. The Lord had us give our entire savings which could have paid for many trips to the islands. Then He gives the trip through these people (whom He later blessed). Everyone received blessing as they first gave. The land was secured and later paid off by the Lord's supply through another individual who approached me.

He said to me, "The Lord has put me here to bless you and the ministry. How can I do this if you do not tell us what you need?" It was the Lord telling me He wants to supply through His people He has blessed so He could bless them more. I needed to get out of the way with my thoughts and just make it clear what the Lord wanted to do.

Elijah had no problem with this when he said, "Give me the first cake and then make one for yourself and your son." When the widow was obedient to that, the supply of God continued for them until the famine ended. When Elijah was obedient to the Lord, then that released the Lord's provision to and through the woman (see 1st Kings 17).

I told the gentleman what we owed on the property and he pulled out his checkbook, wrote a check, and handed it to me. Then he looked at me and said, "What else do you need?"

At other times, the Lord has supplied for His work through other individuals who the Lord raised up to do His purpose and then blessed them. When the devil uses you, he curses you. When the Lord uses you, He blesses you.

As is only fitting, the Holy Spirit would have me take a moment to give thanks to the Lord for all of the faithful people who the Lord has sent to us (past, present, and future). You have proven yourselves so generous and sacrificially been used of the Lord to give as your service to the Lord of your time, talents, encouragement, prayers, and giving your lives and resources! The Lord has blessed you now and in the lifetime to come you have stored up treasures in heaven (Matthew 6)

MINISTRY

If you do not love the people, you have no ministry. The people are the ministry. You and your family are the ministry. It is all about people and relationships. Ministry is allowing the Lord to flow in us and through us on a daily basis. Living life in everyday situations, the Lord meets us where we are. He is concerned about every aspect of our lives. He has a provision for everything we will ever face in life. Life is a daily walk with God and each other, which He wants us to enjoy.

RAISING FAMILY

The most important ministry we have is to our family. As we walk with Jesus, we are to bring them with us.

As I look back in time, I can see how easy it is for people to get involved in the ministry and neglect their own family. The Lord says your first priority of ministry is to disciple your own wife and children. If you do not do this, you have no ministry. (1st Timothy 3:1-7, Titus 1:5-11) (See *God's Order for the Home* book)

I have always believed that what I present to the people of God begins with me. I must be the model or example as I follow Jesus — First to my family and second to the family of God. We are all family, but my first responsibility is to care for my wife and children as the Lord directs, then the people as the Lord directs.

Do not take your family for granted or think they will understand when you sacrifice them over to "care" for someone else. They will forget the hundreds and thousands of times the Lord used you, because of the times they sat in the car waiting or you were not there at their activities.

It is the Lord's ministry. His priority is your life, wife, children, and what pertains to you. He will help you to make certain your "home" base is cared for. Then go minister to the multitudes.

To guard your family is to guard your life. I did not want selfishness, bitterness, or strife in my house. As I mentioned earlier, I could not go to minister to the people if things were not resolved in me or at home.

Boundaries are necessary in all matters of life and relationship. People have to learn what is acceptable and what is not. As in all things God's ways are not man's ways. A godly home should be different than an ungodly home.

"As for me and my house, we will serve the Lord." (Joshua 24:15) In a godly home, ungodly ways and attitudes are not to be permitted. The Lord ordered our home, just like He ordered His church. There are no double standards — home — public. It is all the same.

Children, like the people of God, need consistency and balance as they learn the Lord's ways. They need loving and caring leadership by word and example. (Proverbs 14:26-27; Psalm 129) Parenting is not about the sacrifice of the parents. It is about developing the gift of God in the child.

At the age of two one of the children came up to me lifting her arm and showed me her elbow. Immediately I showed her my elbow. Her response was, "Big elbow." I replied, "And do not forget it." She is growing into a strong courageous leader which is what the Lord called her (Geber) at her birth.

Power plays develop early in children. The Lord always gave Diana and I wisdom in dealing with the children. (James 1)

Another time, around age four, one said to me, "I hate you." I replied, "No, you don't hate me. Is that true?" He nodded. "Is that a yes or a no? I asked. “Yes,” he said. “Do you know why you said that you hate me? He nodded his head. “Is that a yes or a no? He said, “No.” I said, “You said you hate me because I did not let you do what you wanted to do.” He understood. You cannot allow yourself to be emotionally held hostage by your children. They must learn not to be selfish. He grew to be a fine man of God thoughtful and considerate of others.

In Jesse’s first week of preschool he had a little boy come up to him and punch him in the face. The teacher recounted to me that his response was, “You do not love God.” Jesse did not strike him back, but understood that the Lord’s ways are not violence but love, and by the other child’s actions he associated that the child did not love God. It is important that parents teach their children the Lord’s ways by word and example. Jesse was consistent then and he still today is consistent in his manner and behavior seeking to do what the Lord would have him to do, and recognizing when others are doing the Lord’s will or not.

As the children’s parents, Diana and I loved and cared about them more than anyone else on this earth ever could or would. Yet, I would tell them when they could understand, “I am not here to be your friend. I am your dad on an assignment from God to teach and train you in the Lord’s ways so when you get older you will experience the Lord’s best all of your days. What you do in your own life and family later is between you and God. This is the way it is!”

Every night I would pray over the children. One night I came home late and as I was praying over my son, Jesse, he looked at me (he was sound asleep) and said “Hi! Friend.” In his spirit he knew he was my friend and I was his friend even though I had the responsibility to be his Dad.

Diana and I agreed that this is how it would be. As the children both have their own families now, we can look back and say by God’s grace we raised two godly children who we were blessed to have the privilege to raise with no issues because the Lord’s ways work. As they continue to walk in the Lord's ways, their families will be blessed of the Lord as well. We now call them friends.

Each child is different. Each has a different calling and purpose. Each was given a name by the Lord. Both are valuable to the Lord and to us. (See Judges 13:8-12) Both have the same destiny to be with the Lord forever!

Diana and I would both agree that Erin and Jesse have been a gift from the Lord to us. I always thought that I had all the blessings the good Father in heaven gives. Then came the grandchildren — Natalie, Giovanni, Neiko, Lorelai, and Savannah. They all grow up so quickly. Quality time with them is so important. I want to know them and them to know me. Together we will see the Lord's best.

A Servant Of CHRIST

PART 3

APPLICATION

INTRODUCTION

When I turned fifty years of age, the Lord told me several things. One, everything that He had prepared for me in the first fifty years was going to begin to happen. I was entering into the third and final phase of my life and ministry. Secondly, He told me to get a physical every year.

As I look back at life following the Lord's delivering me from my last life threatening car crash (see the Safe Place book). I perceive that all that matters for abundant life living is the moment I am in (with the Lord and whoever and whatever). The past is the past and the future is the future. I am not living in either, so I am enjoying the moment I am in.

I have found that the life with God is a series of adventures in the Word of God and the Holy Spirit in the ongoing saga of life with the Holy Spirit. The Lord goes ahead of us preparing the way (Joshua 1:5-9) He has a provision waiting. Our part is to go with the Lord, trusting (believing) and obeying His word, praising and thanking Him.

We then testify to the Lord's greatness, goodness, faithfulness, forgiveness, and mercy. We tell the people of the wonderful exploits of the Lord's bringing heaven to man, so man might in turn know about believing and receiving the love and life of heaven giving the Lord the praise and the glory for all He has done in Jesus Christ our Lord.

"Let the redeemed of the Lord say so." (Psalm 107:2) Everyone in their lifetime has experiences and stories. Not all of our experiences and

stories line up with the Lord's Word and will. He says, *"My people perish for lack of knowledge."* (Hosea 4:6)

We want to see the Lord's results. This is why we want to have the Lord's truth, knowledge, and wisdom, so we can have His facts, believe Him and get His results for His glory and our good. The Holy Spirit will help us if we ask in faith, believing and relying on Him.

The following stories depict random daily living application in my life of the Lord's presence, promise, wisdom, faith, hope, and love. These stories are intended to increase your confidence in the Lord, His promises, and His presence in your life and ministry. There is nothing too difficult for Him or us in Christ Jesus. Above all, they are intended to give all the glory to the Lord Jesus Christ for all that He has done, is doing, and will do in your and my life forever. We are together forever!

CHILD LIKE FAITH

My two year old daughter's body was racked with pain and congestion. Each time she breathed she would cough and choke. For several days this continued. Since we were believing the Lord for healing in the name of Jesus, I inquired of the Lord why things were not changing. (No parent wants to see their children suffering like this!) No one was sleeping.

I knew Diana and I were believing the Lord but something else was going on. As I inquired of the Lord, He said, "She likes being rocked."

I went to Erin's bedside and said to her, "Erin, Mom and Dad love you. Jesus loves you the most. We all asked Jesus to heal you. His healing is working in you. Mom and Dad will rock you whether you are well or sick."

Within two hours her cough stopped and she was breathing normally. Her desire to be sick and get rocked in the rocking chair had overrode our faith. When I explained to her what the Lord had said was the hindrance and told her that she did not have to be sick to get rocked, she released her faith to be well. She was healed.

STOMACH ACHE

A couple years later I kept hearing Erin talking at night in her bedroom. I asked her, "What is going on?" She said, "Dad the bad one comes at night and makes my stomach hurt."

I instructed her, "Tonight, if the bad one comes, you call to Jesus to help you. Say, "Jesus." That night I heard more conversation going on and I went back to sleep.

The next morning I asked her, "What happened?" She replied, "The bad one came and tried to make my stomach hurt. I said, "Jesus." Jesus came and took the bad one up into the sky." She never had that problem again.

On another occasion, she called me into her room. "Dad," she said very emphatically. "Tell him to quit watching me!"

I looked around and then understood what was going on. Children and animals are often sensitive to the "spirit" realm. "Erin, it is okay," I said. "He is just doing what the Lord has given him (her angel) to do. He watches over you to protect and care for you."

She understood and said, "Okay, Dad." as she pulled the covers over her head.

LOVEY-DOVEY

In our household we have had various pets. Our dove, Lovey-dovey, had fallen from the nest. We prayed over her and Diana nursed it back to health. As the years went by, she was stepped on twice and her wing had been dislocated. Diana wrapped it and we prayed. She was always fine. (Mark 11:22-24)

One day we came home and Lovey-Dovey was lying motionless on the floor. We prayed in Jesus' name. When you pray, believe you have received and you will see it. As several days passed, she appeared to get worse. (This happens to get you to think that your prayer did not work. But in this case it was something different.)

I did not know how long doves lived. My only experience with birds were two parakeets, which, like my fish, did not live over a year. We had Lovey-Dovey for about eight years.

As I sat holding Lovey-Dovey, I did not know whether to release her to the Lord or to believe for life. (My lack of knowledge of what the Lord wanted compromised my faith. (James 1:8) I was double-minded.

The Lord spoke, "Son, do you want her to live or to die?" When I heard that I had a choice, I said, "I want her to live!" The Lord said, "Then speak life into her, in Jesus' name!" I did, and within days she was back to normal. We enjoyed her for another five years.

Later that week, we discovered Lovie-Dovey had been pecking around in one of Diana's "19 plants you cannot kill" called "dumb-cane" which produces a paralysis in the nervous system and could kill you.

NOISE IN THE GARAGE

Diana was thinking that it would be a good thing if I was home more often. When I moved my office to the house, she decided that it would be a better thing if I was not home as much.

We people are funny. We get thoughts and desires that oftentimes are based on our feelings at that moment.

One night early in our marriage there was a crashing sound in the garage which woke Diana up from her sleep. She attempted to wake me up to no avail.

(I am of the thought that the Lord gives His beloved peaceful sleep and we are not to be afraid of the sudden fear (Proverbs 3:21-26). She would say, "When the earthquake happens all Randy does is raise his hand when he is in bed and say, "Stop in Jesus' name.")

Diana expected me to do something. I did. I was sleeping. She took a stick to deal with whatever was in the garage. There was nothing. Something had fallen off the shelf.

As she was returning to bed, the Lord spoke, "See, he is home and he is still worthless. I am your Source and Helper!"

The Lord was not demeaning me, but rather to the contrary He was helping me. Diana had started thinking and relying on me, rather than the Lord. This brought undo pressure and dependency. She is a mighty woman of faith in the Lord. To this day she knows the Lord is her Source and Helper not me.

I woke up the next morning, my shoulder was sore. Before she told me the story and what the Lord had said she said, "Your shoulder is sore because I punched you to wake you up."

THE SPIDER FROM HELL

Sitting at my desk I felt a piercing pain in the back of my leg. I jumped up and with both hands smashed in my pants whatever had bitten me. It was Resurrection Day weekend, and I went on with services as supernaturally normal.

Monday is my "date day" with my bride and we had gone out early for breakfast. All of a sudden my head began swirling with dizziness, fever and chill came over me, and I felt a searing pain in the back of my leg. I went to the restroom and discovered a very hot red spot the size of a half-dollar with a red line going from it up the back of my leg.

From 9:00AM to 4:00PM we spent "date day" in the hospital emergency room. Burning with fever, I placed my hands on my head and from my spirit said, "Father, what am I here for?" (It would have appeared to be obvious why I was there — for me and my condition!) Not two minutes later a man fell on the floor in front of me convulsing and having a seizure. (I had seen him come in with another girl who was sick).

Standing to my feet I commanded "in the name of the Lord Jesus Christ come off and out of him." With the hospital attendants around us, he shook some more and then peace came over him. They took him to the back.

A mother and her teenage son had been talking earlier about receiving Jesus but the boy was having nothing to do with it. Having seen what happened there, he asked his mother to pray with him to receive Jesus as his Lord and Savior.

A while later we were called to the back. My fever was gone. The nurse thanked us for our patience. The doctor came in and thanked us for caring for his patient and asked me to drop my pants. I was watching Diana's expression as the doctor asked, "What is the problem? I see nothing but a pin prick."

The Lord had healed me and it was all gone! The Lord had us there that day on His assignment for other things which He wanted us to do. I tell people it is not about you and what you are going through. Ask the Lord what He wants to do in the circumstance and situation you are in. You are in His care and hands. What else is the Lord doing?

We would never have been in that place to do what the Lord accomplished through us if it were not for the bite (which occurred on

Friday) but did not manifest until Monday (not normal reaction) but the assignment was for Monday.

OOZING SORES

A young man received the prayer of faith in the prayer line for crusty oozing sores. A few weeks later when I saw him, nothing had changed, so I asked the Lord, "Is there something hindering his healing or some further instruction?" The Lord said, "Tell him to go to the beach, sit in the sun, go in salt water, and to rest."

I told him what I was given. He listened and then said, "I believe when we prayed I was healed." (It was like he was saying, "Where is your faith, Pastor?") We walk by faith and not sight, but there was something else.

Unknown to me, his employer was telling him that he needed to go see a doctor. He refused. Now they were telling him that if he did not go see the doctor he would be fired from his job because you cannot deal with the public with oozing sores.

Economics are a motivator. When he went to the doctor, the doctor told him, "Go to the beach, and sit in the sun and saltwater, and rest." Within weeks his skin was completely healed. (All the authorities in his life were in agreement.)

Seeking forgiveness, he returned to me. He confessed his worry, stubbornness, and rebellion to the authorities in his life.

The oozing sores were not the problem or issue. There were underlying issues which the Lord was dealing with related to honoring the Lord and His authorities who are there for his good.

FEED MY BIRDS

In our yard the birds of the air truly never needed to labor for their food. Diana always fed them. (Matthew 6)

As I was looking at our cherry trees one day, I noticed that the birds had again eaten them all. The Lord spoke to me, "Son, what are you doing?" (The Lord knows what I am doing. He wants me to know what I am doing.)

I replied, "I am complaining because the birds ate all of the cherries again," (so I did not get any). (Proverbs 16:2) *"A man's ways appear right to a man, the Lord searches the motivation of the heart."*

The issue was not that the birds ate all the cherries, but rather that I did not get any — no not one for all the effort I had put in pruning, fertilizing, watering, etc.

The Lord spoke again, "Son, who cares for you?" I replied, "Father, You care for me. You care for me very well!"

There was a pause as the Lord let me listen to my words. Then He spoke again, "Then, son, you take care of My birds."

Over the next several weeks, the Lord put it on people's hearts and they kept bringing me cherries. So many cherries came to me that I had to give them away to others.

SPRINKLERS

I have been blessed with children who do whatever they do with all their heart in the name of Jesus to the glory of God. They are both excellent workers who work hard at what they do. They are committed and responsible. Because of this I could not figure out why it was that when my son was doing the yard work everything was done perfectly, except he would not mow around the fence. Jesse is an obedient son with a gentle heart. I would tell him to be sure to mow that area, but it was not mowed.

I asked the Lord, "What is wrong? Why won't he mow that area?" The Lord said, "He is afraid to break the sprinklers." (I would get upset.)

My heart was sad because I realized how hard I was on him about breaking the sprinklers. I went to him and said, "Son, I do not care how many sprinklers you break. Just mow down that area. We will fix the sprinklers together."

There never was a problem again. After that we did not really have to fix many sprinklers again, except the next day when I broke six.

IF YOU ARE HEALED

There was a four year period in my life when the Lord was teaching me about how His healing works and what is all involved in the spirit, mind, and body. The three are all related in the Lord's healing. "Which is easier to say, 'Your sins are forgiven' or 'Take up your bed and walk.' " (Matthew 9:5)

As often occurs when you are learning something in life, you are proved or tested. I was learning about healing, so I got sick. I was in my bed when the Lord spoke to me, "Son, what are you doing?" (He always knows what I am doing (Psalm 137) He wants me to know).

I replied, "Lord, I am confessing my healing." (I was quoting the healing scriptures "By His stripes I am healed," etc. He asked me, "Do you believe you are healed?" "Yes," I responded. There was a pause. He asked again, "What would you normally be doing this time of the day?" (It was afternoon.) I answered, "I would not be lying in bed. I would be about your business." There was another pause.

The Lord's response to this statement was, "Son, if you are healed, then get up out of bed and be about My business!"

To receive the Lord's results we must obey what He says to do whether we understand it or feel it or not. I immediately got out of bed. I was still dizzy and nauseous and fell into the closet. I got up, washed my face, and went in to tell Diana that I was going out to the nursing home.

The people at the home ministered to me more that day then I ministered to them. When I came home, I was completely healed and ate a great dinner that Diana had prepared for me.

You can confess scriptures and pray all day long for healing or anything else, but until you act on your healing you will not be healed. This is what I learned that day from the Lord about faith.

TO BE CRIPPLED OR NOT
(Part 1)

A man stood before me in a prayer line. I started shouting at him, "You are not a cripple. Do not believe or receive that you are a cripple." (He had three major back surgeries. The doctors were now telling him that he would be a cripple. I did not know this, but the Lord did.) "Run with me," I commanded. He said, "I can't!" "In Jesus' name, run with me. You are not a cripple!" He started to run and his wife jumped from her seat to stop him. (The fears of others will hinder your faith.) The ushers stopped her as she watched her husband running with me.

He was running with me, yet the infirmity spirit that was on him was cursing God and me as he ran. (It has to go in Jesus' name!) As we ran together back the other way, the spirit left him. He was not a cripple, nor ever would be a cripple to the glory of God. His wife was greatly encouraged.

(Part 2)

The man that was redeemed by the Lord from being a cripple did not know that he was part of God's larger plan that day. As you recall, I said to him, "Run with me." The Lord was telling me to run with him. Neither one of us in the Lord's plan was to be a cripple.

Months prior I was involved in a basketball mishap in which someone had tripped and fallen on my heal which caused me to fall forward. It was like an axe chopped my leg. All the tendons and muscles snapped in the back of my leg. Pain beyond pain. (Some things in life happen suddenly — not because of sin, or attacks of the devil, but because of accidents. No worry, the Lord knew it would happen and has a plan and a provision.)

The game stopped. The believers prayed in Jesus' name. (John 14:12-14) I was carried off the court. I sought to act on my healing, but could not stand. I inquired of the Lord what to do. He said, "Soak the leg in hot Epson salt." (Monday).

Tuesday we had services so I went to church. I never had the thought that I would be a cripple. I walked on the leg for the next months, but there was no spring or jump. It was like a stump. Nevertheless, when Jesse would say, "Dad, would you like to play basketball?" I would say, "Sure, son, let's play." There was no jump, but I knew the Lord had and was healing me. I was not a cripple.

My medical friends told me that even if I had had a surgery or two there were no guarantees of the leg returning to full use. I knew whom I had believed (2nd Timothy 1:12). The Lord had and was working His healing in me. I could not tell you the exact moment of the manifestation of the spring and jump that came back into my leg, but it did even though the tendons remained disconnected and the muscles were never reattached.

STRETCHING FAITH

GNARLED HAND

A man came to the prayer line for a hand that had been caught in a machine. I started to pray over his hand and the Lord said, "Stop. Ask him what he wants." I asked him, and he said, "I am believing to be able to use my hand again."

It is important to know what people are believing for. *"Be it done to you according to your faith."* In many cases, they are believing for less than what the Lord has for them.

I said to the man, "Sir, I am believing that your hand will be as good as new." He thought, and said, "That's what I want." We believed the Lord.

A few weeks later he was at service again. He came up to me all excited, "Pastor, the last time I was here I learned about tithes and offerings. I gave my first tithe that day. The next week I received a pay increase, a new place to live, and a better car.

I asked him, "What about your hand?" "Oh, I forgot about that. It is as good as new!" We give to you the praise and glory, Lord Jesus.

DYING OF EMPHYSEMA

A lady came for prayer who was given a month to live. She was dying of emphysema. She was not a smoker. Her husband was a smoker (he died of lung cancer and emphysema). Secondary smoke was what was killing her.

I asked her, "What do you want?" She said, "In my last days, I want to just be able to breathe better."

Looking at her I said, "That is not what you want. You want the lungs of a little child."

She exclaimed, "That is what I want!"

She asked the doctor for another x-ray. When the results came back, the doctor told her, "You have the lungs of a little child." Praise the Lord!

1/2 INCH MORE

In the prayer line I asked a lady to remove her shoe which had a five inch lift. As the Lord touched her in Jesus' name, her leg grew out 4 ½ inches in a minute and a half.

I felt a pain in my chest and I asked the lady, "Why did you stop your faith?" She says to me, "Pastor, some things take a while to happen."

I told her, "Your leg grew 4 ½ inches in a minute and a half. Why can't we give it another minute?"

"No," she replied. "Some things take a while to happen." She walked out carrying her shoe with the five inch lift.

I do not believe it was her faith that caused her leg to grow 4 ½ inches in a minute and a half, but rather God's gift. However, I do believe that it was her false knowledge and understanding that prevented the Lord from finishing the ½ inch more.

SIMPLE FAITH

In the early years of Glory to God I received a call from a man whose wife was terminally ill with cancer. He had heard about what the Lord was doing and asked me to come and pray for his wife.

As I was speaking with him, I had a vision of him asking me, "What does it mean to be born again?" I received nothing about his wife. We finished the conversation and set up an appointment.

I always bring someone with me. We were welcomed into his home. He brought us to his wife and we prayed over her. As Jesus felt power go from him, I felt nothing. She was not receiving anything. (People sometimes want you to pray over someone who is really not believing for change or even wants the prayer.)

As an act of her faith, I asked her to get up and wash her face when we left the room, but she was quick to say, "No, I am too sick. I cannot do that."

Her husband ushered us to the other room to sit with him on the sofa. The first thing he said, "What does it mean to be born again?" (His neighbor had been talking to him about Jesus).

He received the love of God and Jesus as his Lord and Savior. We baptized him with water and the Holy Spirit. He was speaking in tongues and praising God. We left.

This became a monumental test for me. A few days later I was sick and praying in my prayer spot and a voice spoke to me, "Physician, you have healed others, why can't you heal yourself?"

I had just read in the obituary that the lady had died. I was sick and I had some demonic thing taunting and mocking me and my faith in God. It was attempting to stop me from believing the Lord and praying for others by telling me that it does not work.

I rose up in the Holy Spirit and told it, "Get out of here in the name of Jesus Christ!" Then the Lord ministered to me, "Son, go back to the man and get all the facts!" I will never forget this. Get all the facts! What was going on? What was the woman believing, etc.?

I went and he welcomed me and sat me down. He proceeded to tell me that the next day his wife had told him to gather the family because she wanted to talk to them before she died. They did so and she died.

She never intended to live, nor did she even want the prayer. She was just being kind to her husband, permitting his desire to take place. I learned that the prayer of faith is good. It will work, if people want it to work. What the Lord had shown me happened. I do not just pray over or for anyone anymore except I know what they are believing and that the prayer is directed by the Father's will. Specifically, I do not pray that the person live or die, but that they finish what the Father gives them to do in this lifetime.

PAINFUL FEET

I heard the door in the rear auditorium slam shut. A lady had just angrily stomped out of the service. For 30 to 40 minutes she had stood in the prayer line that day. Each time I came to her, the Holy Spirit would have me tell her, "Just be patient, ma'am, the Lord has something for you today." Then I would go on to pray for the next person.

As she left, the Lord had me say to the people, "If you cannot stand and wait for what the Lord has for you, you will not ever receive what He has for you." Through faith and patience we receive all the promises of God. Be strong in the Lord. Having done all to stand, stand in the Lord.

You can always tell a piece of hate mail. We had one come from this woman the next week. It stated that I was the most inconsiderate, unloving, insensitive minister that she had ever met and possibly I was not even saved.

I asked the Lord if I should respond and what I should do. He said to send her a tape, "Overcoming the impossible." The flipside was entitled "Jairus' daughter." People who have listened to and believed this tape have experienced mighty significant miracles.

The next week the woman came in late to church, walked down front and sat right in front of me. She raised her hand.

"Lord, do you want me to acknowledge her?" "Yes." He replied. She said to the people, "I want to testify. This morning I went to see my friend. When I attempted to get out of the car, I could not. A voice spoke to me, 'Turn on the radio.' I turned it on and Pastor Randy's program was on. I listened to it and then tried to get out of the car again with no success. I heard the voice again, "Go to the service." Here I am. I have been over the years all over the country to every healing evangelist and meeting seeking healing for my bone condition which I was born with. (She had a bone condition which caused her to not walk or stand for long periods of time without excruciating pain.)

She continued, "I have had no results. I did not know how to receive my healing nor how to wait (patience) for my healing. Pastor Randy was the only one who forced me to act on my healing. He did not pray, but forced me to stand even though I was in great pain. I know today when hands are laid on me, I will receive my healing." We put hands on her in Jesus' name. She started jumping and shouting and then ran around the room. Glory to God!

CLOSE THE MEETINGS

The Lord had been touching me about the power of the blood of Jesus and its protective quality (Passover event, etc.). Teaching is no good without application. So I put the blood of Jesus over everyone and everything.

One day I spoke it over the door frames to a meeting hall that we were in. However, I made a mistake. I said that anyone who is not of God cannot come in. The crowd diminished.

One person told me later that he had come to the door and could not come in. The next week I prayed that anyone who was not of God and wanted to get free could come in, and the place filled back up.

During the next week's service a man came late into service and stood right in my face challenging me. He turned to the people and shouted, "I am sent from the devil to stop these meetings. I am to tell you to go back to your dead churches and quit coming here." He turned to challenge me.

I have two angels the Lord has given to me. The one on the left (the protector) picked the man up and threw him eight feet onto the floor. I then said, "The blood of Jesus covers all of us! In Jesus' name, you cannot use him anymore!"

The man repented of his unforgiveness towards his mother and was free as the demon left him. *"Submit yourself to God, resist the devil and he will flee from you."* (James 4:7) The man's unforgiveness towards his mother opened a door to a devil to use him (see Ephesians 4:26-28).

When he confessed his sin (getting under the blood of Jesus and submitted to God), he was forgiven, delivered, and then testified what great things the Lord had done for him.

GROWLING CONGREGANT

As I was ministering the Word of the Lord which brings healing, a man in the crowd started to growl and curse. The Holy Spirit in the house brought to manifestation the devils that were in this man.

He used to be a bar brawler before Jesus came into his life. This day the Holy Spirit was delivering him. He stood up and started throwing chairs. Six men could not contain him.

Walking towards him, hand extended, I spoke "You are bound in Jesus' name." He could not move. When I put my finger on his chest, I said, "You are weak and he is free of you in Jesus' name!" He slumped to the ground and has been free ever since. Praise the Lord. Authority over all the power of the devil (Luke 10:19-20)

ENCOUNTER IN THE PARK

At 2:00AM, I received a call from a drunk ranting and raving man. He was telling me he did not like what I (really the Lord) had done to his wife. She was different. He was cursing God, combative, and disturbing my sleep.

I said, "I will see you in the park at 10:00AM." I hung the phone up.

When I drove up at 10:00AM, he was already sitting at a park bench next to his motorcycle with a half empty case of beer. As I approached him, he was shouting obscenities and threats about how he was going to beat me up, etc. He just kept drinking more beer for another half hour.

Then he said something I thought was very interesting. "You must know something. I can't figure out why I haven't beat you up by now (polite version). You must know Karate. You are not afraid of me."

I remained standing there. Calm because I knew the Lord's angels were around me (Psalm 91).

Then he said, "There is something around you." At that, I responded, "The Lord Jesus is with me and His angels protect me. The Lord loves you and I did not come to fight you. The Lord wants me to love you! May I sit down with you and let's talk?"

He had finished the case of beer and motioned to me to come over and sit down.

For over an hour we talked about the love of Jesus and he received Jesus into his heart as Lord and Savior. We prayed that he would receive the peace, joy, and love of God and turn from violence and anger.

He left me at the table and told me he would be back. After a while he brought others from the park that he wanted to experience what he had. This went on all afternoon.

Months later I received a call from the Sheriff's department. He had been in a horrible motorcycle accident. Eight officers could not hold him down so they could get him into the ambulance.

I was the only one he wanted to speak with. He wanted the prayer of peace. The Lord healed him and he went on to lead a productive life.

SOARING INTO THE HEAVENLIES

Before I go to sleep, I ask the Lord to protect us and the Lord's people and to minister to us by His Spirit while we sleep. On this one particular night I found myself soaring into the heavenlies.

There was beautiful light and colors. How indescribable was the peace, joy, and love! I wanted to stay there.

I kept hearing an annoying voice say to me, "Go back! Go back! You don't know where you are going!"

I ignored the voice. What did I care if I did not know where I was going. I kept soaring. It was so awesomely wonderful!

The next day I was meeting with some pastors, and some of them were discussing how God is light and other virtues of the Lord from a conference they had attended. I just sat there still caught up in the fact that I have participated in such a heavenly experience.

Later that day, the Lord ministered to me that it was my spirit by the Holy Spirit that was soaring in the presence of the Lord. It was my mind that kept annoying me by attempting to limit me and hold me back to my own understanding. In the Lord my spirit has no bounds if I do not let my mind bind me. This applies also to my old flesh, world, and demonic influence.

The Lord gave me the verse Ephesians 3:20 *"Now to Him who is able to do far more exceedingly abundantly more than anything that we are able to ask or think according to the power that works in us* (the same power that raised Jesus from the dead) — *to Him be the glory in the church."*

Another time the Lord ministered something very similar.

ICE ON THE OFF RAMP

As I was driving off the freeway on the off ramp, I lost control of the car. It spun and I was going backward over the cliff. My mind was screaming, "you're going to die! You're going to die!" All of a sudden from my spirit I yelled out, "Jesus!"

The car that was spinning out of control suddenly stopped. It was like the Lord just put His hand on the car and held it.

My heart was pounding as I sat there. The Lord spoke, "Son, while you were doing all your fancy driving techniques I could not help you. But when you spoke My name, I stepped in!"

What the Lord was teaching me was that as long as I was leaning to my own understanding and resources He could not help me. It was my spirit that called to God. My mind was telling me, "You are going to die!" (Proverbs 3:5-6) The Lord had other plans.

FIRE ON THE MOUNTAIN

Jesus spoke to the storm, "Peace be still," and it calmed. To them that believe the works I do you will do in My name. (John 14:12-14; James 5:13-16)

We have seen the Lord do these weather phenomena workings many times. Whether bringing the rain, stopping the storm, changing the wind, or cooling the temperatures, etc. the Lord has given to the believer authority over the elements.

In southern California we have many fires. Many are caused by people who want to do others harm. The winds blow with great velocity at certain times of the year.

On one such occasion Diana called me, "They are evacuating the area! What should I do?" The Lord revealed to me that "He was on the mountain." Do not fear. Stay there!"

A sixty foot high wall of fire swept across the area traveling several miles in minutes. The Lord protected all of the homes. (Psalm 107:28-31)

Another time, as our neighbor stated, "It is all lost." The Lord turned the wind, at our request in Jesus' name right before the wall of fire was going to burn down all the homes. Everyone was safe.

No evil or any plague shall come near me or my dwelling. (Psalm 91) Many times the Lord has turned the wind back onto the fire snuffing it out because it cannot breath.

LIFE SAVER

I kissed my daughter as she went away on a school field trip. An apprehension came over me as the bus drove off. That night as I was dreaming I saw her as a little girl under the water with bubbles coming out of her nose as she floated back to the top of the pool. I fished her out, as I had so many times before.

In the dream, however, she stayed under the water. I jumped out of bed and prayed in the Spirit (tongues). The Lord knows everything. Praying in the Spirit the Lord gave me what to pray for before it happened to change what was intended for evil to good to His glory. (Romans 8:26-28)

The next day Erin was white water rafting. The raft flipped over. She was caught under the raft with a heavy classmate on top of her. She nearly drowned, but the Lord intervened, saving her life.

This type of working has occurred many times over the years. Praying the tongues by the Holy Spirit is the Lord's supernatural tool to help us deal with demonic attacks of which we are not aware.

NO PLUMBING

A woman came forward for prayer who was not able to have children. Prayer in the name of Jesus was done and hands were laid upon her. She was filled with the Holy Spirit with the evidence of speaking in tongues.

What we did not know was that she did not have all the body parts necessary for childbearing. The Lord did a creative miracle for her and she had a healthy baby girl.

DEATH WISH

The Lord revealed to me in a dream a woman in the congregation. She was holding in her hand the placenta of an unborn child rejoicing in the child's death. In the dream I was appalled by what I saw.

The next day I went to her and asked her, "Do you want this baby?" (She had multiple children and was tired and depressed that she was pregnant again.) She said, "No, I wished it to die!" (She had already begun signs of losing the baby.) She was weeping.

The Lord told her through us, "Repent and you must receive the child with joy!" She confessed her sin and the Lord forgave her.

Months later when she delivered the child, the child was born dead. The placenta, instead of being rich with red blood, was grey ashen looking and crumbled when touched.

The woman remembered the Word of the Lord, "Receive the child with joy." As she held the lifeless child in her arms, she began to praise and thank the Lord for the Lord's goodness giving her another son. As she celebrated the Lord and her son rejoicing and receiving him with joy, the Lord breathed life into the precious little boy.

DISTRACTIONS

The Lord always has prospered everything which we have set our hand to do. However, we found out in our early ministry years that every vision or agenda that people approached us about was not for us to do.

Our desire to help others fulfill their vision, or their desire to have us help them fulfill their vision, (which was more often the case) posed problems for us fulfilling the vision which the Lord had given us to do.

For three years we operated a grade school. It was growing and very successful. The only problem was that it was depleting funds which were necessary for the ministry's vision. The school was the vision of others, not the vision of the ministry. The Lord provides for the vision He gave you, not for someone else's vision.

When we discontinued the school, and channeled the children to other schools, the ministry flourished again.

You can not be swayed from the vision the Lord has given to you by the agendas and opinions of others, or to help fill needs and desires of others. Nor should we try to be like or do things the way others do them. We must be faithful to do what the Lord has given to us in the way He wants to do it — no more or less!

EMPTY STAGE

The Lord told me one day, "Let them graze in the pasture." He was speaking about our singers and musicians. Ego and resulting strife had made them complicated. Personal desires had become more important than simply worshipping the Lord. The Lord knew that.

Within several weeks of sitting them out, they were near all gone. The Lord must have known something that I did not know.

He said, "Son, if you love what you are doing more than the one you are doing it for — it is worth nothing (vanity). These people were not part of the Lord's ministry team. They were only there because they loved singing and playing for themselves. (Proverbs 16:2) People change over time (just like Lucifer).

Worship to the Lord is not entertainment for the people or the entertainer. The Lord wants those who would worship Him in Spirit and in Truth. He also wants the proper personnel who are one in heart and mind about the vision of the ministry which the Lord has given to you to do. (2nd Chronicles 5:11-14)

I tell people, "Just be honest with me. Are you here to fulfill and get equipped for the ministry the Lord has given you to do elsewhere, or are you here to work with us as a team and to fulfill the vision in this place? This is real important for you and them to know if you are going to work together.

"Whatever you do, do it with all your heart, in the name of Jesus, to the glory of God. (Colossians, Philippians)

BREAKING OUT OF THE EGG

In nature whatever the creature is that is in the egg, if it is assisted in getting out of the egg, it is less likely to survive in life. Character, stamina, and other overcoming qualities are developed during this significant process of life and development.

In ministry it is the same way. Upon many occasions over the years I have had people approach me about setting them up in TV, radio, and various ministries. They wanted us to finance and do it for them.

Our response is always the same. "If the Lord has called and anointed you to do something, you will have to do it the same way we did — seek the Lord with all your heart — believe and obey the Lord — and love and care for the people. The Lord will bring to pass what He has for you." (John 6:37)

GENUINE CARE

As the day of the Lord is approaching, the Lord is raising up ministers of His own heart who have a genuine care for the people. He told me to do three things. "Love My people — care for My people — for I am coming soon!"

The thought has always been in my heart that *If you are not willing to minister in a nursing home, then you probably do not have a ministry.* This is real care for the people who can do nothing in return to you (so people think).

Jesus talks often about caring for and inviting the people who can not benefit you. Paul says, "I have no one else (on the ministry team) like Timothy who has a genuine care for the people." (Philippians 2)

If you want to be a minister of God, you must have a real love for the people, not the ministry and what you do, but, a genuine love for the people. They are the ministry.

INCIDENTS

A man came to me and said, "You think you are going to be famous." I responded, "I will be everything the Lord has determined me to be in His plan and Kingdom." "No man can take to himself something the Lord has not given." (John 3:27) What the Lord has given and will give is on the way. Be confident of that fact — the Lord is with and for you. Love the Lord and His people. Obey the Lord. Destroy the devil's work. (Acts 10:38)

Discouragement tried to come concerning "were there not ten healed and one comes back to give thanks to God." The Lord replied, "son, thank and praise Me that ten were healed. Thank Me that one did come back and give thanks to Me."

The Lord told me that He had given to me the "garbage detail." (We take the people's worst moments, fears, sin, and trash away. In return bring heaven to them in Jesus' name!) I tell people, "I am the garbage man, not the garbage can. Do not dump or vomit on me."

I thank the Lord that He gives strength for the day. He occupies my time with gladness of heart. (Ecclesiastes 5:20) The joy of the Lord is my strength. (Nehemiah 8:10)

A fellow said to me, "You do not take life seriously. You are too happy." I replied, "You do not know me or what I deal with everyday. I rejoice in the Lord always (Philippians 4:4) and He gives to me strength and wisdom to deal with life and overcome."

"Are you a Christian?" I asked. He said, "Yes I am." Then you should be rejoicing in the Lord always as well." He agreed.

Jesus did not consider the contradiction of the cross for the joy that was set before Him. (Hebrews 12:1-3) The Lord will turn what is intended for evil into good to His glory. I know whom I have believed. (2nd Timothy 1:12)

"Pastor, you do not listen," a man said to me. I replied, "Not true. I heard everything you said." (I repeated it to him). I continued, "What you said was not of God and I do not agree with what you said." Some people equate listening with agreement obeying. I did not agree with him so he thought I did not listen to him. Stand up for truth and do not be intimidated by the people. Shepherd who follows sheep steps in stuff.

A man asked me, "Pastor, what can I do for you?" I replied, "Be faithful." In the weeks following he led a rebellion in the church which failed because the Lord will fight for His own who honor Him.

He would have been wise to follow the Lord's Word to him about faithfulness. The Lord was giving him an opportunity to not do what was in his heart to do so he could be blessed and not cursed by his own actions.

"Many profess unfailing love, but a faithful servant who can find?" (Proverbs) "You betray Me with a kiss Judas?" (Luke 22:48)

Many people lack vision and faith. A pastor is to lead the congregation. A man said, "Pastor, we will have to cross that bridge when we get to it." My response, "The way we are going we will never get to that bridge to cross it." Speak the Truth in love so people can grow up in the faith and will of God. (Ephesians 4:14-16)

QUIET MOMENTS

The finest joy in my life has been the quiet times of worship and prayer in the Lord's presence. I love being with the Lord's people as we worship and pray together in community.

In those "alone" moments with the Lord is where I have found rest and forgiveness, strength and renewal, correction and assurance, direction and guidance, comfort, healing and freedom.

As I would pour my heart out to the Lord about the care of the people, fulfilling His will, and the miracles of the situations that arise in life, family, and the ministry, the Lord would show His faithfulness and give to me whatsoever I was needing — I can truly say, "The Lord has been good to me. I have never lacked for any good thing because of His supply. All that He has said, He has done! Praise be the Lord now and forevermore."

The "hearing ear" and the "instructed tongue" (Isaiah) is what Jesus had and what I sought after from the Lord that I might know, speak, and do His will. Jesus never said or did anything that His Father had not given Him to say or do. (John 8:28-30) Trust is the desire of my heart as well that the Father take pleasure in, be honored and glorified in and through me in the name of Jesus.

One day in such a quiet time, the Lord gave me a simple song, "Lead me, Lord. Lead me in your righteousness. Make your ways known to me O Lord."

GOD'S REST

For years I was so busy about the care of the people that I would not take time off. This was effecting me and my marriage. One day the Lord said, "Push off the boat!" He left the multitudes on the beach and went to the other side of the lake.

He took a break from the ministry for personal refreshing (see *God's Rest* book). This was a practice that Jesus did often. The Lord taught me that if I was not taking care of myself, how could I take care of His people. He even rested on His Sabbath.

Often after a major spiritual accomplishment occurs, an attack will come. We had just completed a TV series on emotions which has helped set free countless people over the years. Driving home a truck in front of me hit a pipe on the road launching the pipe through my windshield with such force that the authorities thought a sniper had shot a bullet at my windshield.

The Lord used the mirror to deflect the pipe which proceeded to blow out my driver side window. (The investigators could not figure out how I was still alive.) (Psalm 91) The mirror struck my face breaking my palate, both jaws, puncturing a hole in my cheek, and rearranging my teeth.

Immediately, I asked the Lord, "Am I out of your will?" I saw His mighty right hand. I knew I was in His care (Psalm 91). If I had not been in His will, I would have asked for forgiveness and got back in His will. (James 4:7)

The Lord said, "What was intended for evil, I will turn for good. Be patient, son." "Let them set the teeth and I will cement them!" The Lord did what He said! At the time of this book, 27 years later, everything is perfect. The Lord be praised!!

This is such an amazing testimony of God's faithfulness you will need to read the entire account of what and how the Lord was glorified through this testimony of faith, time, and patience (*Patience* book).

Through faith and patience we will inherit all the promises of God! The Lord was revealing how He can take us through the mountain when it does not move right away (Mark 11:22-25).

THE SAFE PLACE
(See *Safe Place* book)

In March a year before the events of 9/11 happened in America at New York throwing the entire world into a trouble and terror alert this event occurred in my life to the glory of God.

Following a wonderful time of fellowship and encouragement with some other ministers, we drove off. I was the third one driving across the intersection. Driving through a red light at great speed a car struck me on my driver side door.

Instantly, I found myself in a very quiet, peaceful, and happy place. (Totally different from the witness reports of what was actually happening to the car and myself.) It took twenty minutes to cut me out of the demolished car with the "Jaws of Life."

Six hours later I awoke in the hospital. Nothing was wrong and there was not even a cut. When I thanked the doctor he pointed up with his finger. He knew he had experienced a miracle.

Asking the Lord if I had died, He replied, "No, son, the thief tried to take your life again (referring to the pipe incident), but I took you with Me to the 'Safe Place.'" Later, He proceeded to teach me about the "Safe Place" in Him. "I want you to tell the whole world about the 'Safe Place' free of trouble and terror."

This occurred one year before 9/11 in America. I have found that as people learned about the safe place they were protected from bullets, land mines, car crashes, falling off buildings, etc.

The testimony and teaching to God's glory about the Safe Place is recorded in *The Safe Place* book.

BE IN THE SPIRIT — IN THE MOMENT

Following the Safe Place accident the Lord taught me about what I consider one of the most important keys to life. Paul talks about a key or secret to life as being contentment (Philippians 4:11-13) in whatever situation of life you are experiencing.

A great thankfulness appears to overcome people who have experienced the safe place and other fulfilled promises of God. A great contentment accompanies this thankfulness.

The Lord told me, "Be (exist) in the Spirit (of God) in the moment (you are in). Do not think about the past or the future for you are not existing there."

He was teaching me another key to the abundant life Jesus promised (John 10:10). Many people do not know how to enjoy their life. The Lord was saying be thankful and enjoy every moment He gives you life. The past moments are past. The future moments have not yet come. You are not there in the past or the future, so it profits nothing to seek to be there or think and dwell on those things.

You are in this moment with the Lord, yourself, and whoever you are with. Enjoy this moment and make the most of this moment in the Lord's Spirit! In the Lord's presence or spirit is fullness of Joy (Psalm 16:11).

JUST SLEEPING

When the people came to Jairus saying, 'Don't trouble Jesus about your daughter. She is dead." Jesus replied, "Jairus, do not fear. Only believe." He went on to tell the people she is just sleeping." They laughed at Jesus because they knew she was dead.

Like Paul in the Acts we have seen the Lord raise up two people who died while in the church service. In both instances medical people attended to and pronounced both people to have died. However, the Lord had other plans that He might be glorified. In Jesus' name they were both brought back to life.

The one, as I said to the people, "She is just sleeping" — she began to snore very loudly as the Lord restored life to her. She later prayed over everyone to remove their fear that had been traumatized by her sudden death.

GOING TO HELL

Years earlier my wife's dad had died in the hospital of heart conditions. Through the prayer of faith in the name of Jesus to the glory of God, he was raised back to life. Previously we were believing for his salvation. I said to the Lord, "Father, he is going to hell. You need to save him. The Lord did it. He came alive again. His heart was healed. He was born again confessing and receiving Jesus as his Lord and Savior. He was water baptized and filled with the Holy Spirit speaking in tongues. Many years later when Jesus picked him up to take him home, there was nothing physically wrong with him.

HOVER OVER THE NEST

My wife was to go into the hospital and have a "minor" after the babies lady surgery. The Lord said, "Son, hover over the nest."

The surgery went fine and they moved her into a room. As I was sitting there watching over her as she slept, something happened. Her blood pressure started to plummet. The blood was running out of her.

The hospital attendants rushed in and attempted to defibulate her to get her heart going again. It did not work.

I removed everyone out of the room. "In the name of Jesus spirit of death get off of her. What is causing this blood loss cease! Blood pressure and life come back to her!" I said as I lay across her body.

Warmth started to come back into her body and her color started to change. Minutes later she opened her eyes and said to me, "You look a mess."

The doctor rejoiced with us in what the Lord had done. Apparently, something had been cut inside her which was causing her to bleed out into her womb. The Lord turned what was intended for evil to good to His glory.

As Diana recounts the story, "All of a sudden things around became very quiet. (She would put her hands over her ears as she told the story.) She was in a very warm place. (Her body was cold because of the great blood loss). It was bright, warm sand, turquoise water. She said to the Lord, "Father, if it is my time to go, I am ready. But the children are young and Randy is going to need help with them. If you want me to stay I would like to stay because I do not want Randy to remarry." She then opened her eyes.

All day I continued to do what the Lord had told me. "Hover over the nest." Come night Diana rolled over looking at me she said, "It is Tuesday. Aren't you supposed to be at church?" I replied, "No, love you are my assignment."

Over the years, I believe that meant more to her that I was "hovering over the nest," than many other things in life. So often she had sacrificed her life for the people and now the Lord was looking out for her.

I tell her your rewards when Jesus comes back are probably going to be greater than mine. You have devoted your life to the Lord and enabled both of us together to be about our Father in Heaven's business. We are together with God's people — Jesus' team. Blessed!

ASSIGNMENTS

Divine appointments and assignments have filled my life. The Lord said, "We will reach the world one person at a time."

One such assignment led me to go back to school. I have had twenty four years of formal education. It was not about receiving honors and degrees. It was about that the Lord wanted me in that place during that time to accomplish His purpose for others and myself.

As I was flying back to school the Lord spoke, "A student is not greater than the teacher." The Lord wanted me to remember my place. Although I had more education and ministry experience than many, I was on His assignment and submitted to the working.

Iron sharpens iron — brothers can sharpen each other. I received from them under the Lord's direction. Professors were filled with the Holy Spirit and given life counsel. I was learning and growing with peers. It was a rich blessing for all. Friendships have continued to this day because of the Lord's assignment and appointment.

The Lord always wants to accomplish many purposes through what He does. In this case, it was not about degree, but relationship and obedient assignment. Knowledge puffs up — love builds up. (1st Corinthians 8:1-3) People to see — things to do. The Lord was also taking me out of one environment of negativity and putting me in an environment of growth.

THIEF IN THE CAMP
(The Lucifer Spirit)

In ministry often times the people do not appreciate the gift of God in their minister. This occurs when they start thinking more highly of themselves than they ought to. They do not recognize their place, but rather think they are equal to and better than their minister of God.

This was Lucifer's sin. His spirit oftentimes gets on the people and causes others to depreciate the minister of God and attempt to take over the ministry. (God-Lucifer/Moses-Miriam and Aaron, Moses-Korah and elders, etc. — Self promoters.

As I mentioned earlier in the book, a person approached me asking the question, "What can I do for you, Pastor?" My reply was, "Be faithful to God, yourself, my family and I, and to the ministry." Two weeks later he is a leading part of those seeking to take over the ministry.

Ministers of God remember this: The Lord will be with you and destroy the work of the devil. Lucifer was kicked out of heaven and Miriam received leprosy. Korah and the leaders of Israel were consumed, etc. No weapon formed against you will prosper (Isaiah 54:17, 41:9-13, Psalm 18).

This is what I call the Lucifer spirit. It has raised its head periodically over the years only to be exposed, and violently removed by the Lord. Horrible things have happened to those who oppose the Lord and His servants. It is true what the Lord says, "Touch not My anointed!"

Stay out of it! You do not need to defend yourself. The Lord will stand up for you! Focus on going about the Lord's business caring and loving the people. Everything will show itself for what it is. Time is your friend.

TIME TO MOVE

While resting in my lounge chair following resurrection day services, the Lord spoke, "It is time to move!"

Diana and I by the Lord's provision and direction had just finished repairing, fixing up the home that the Lord had enabled us to have years before. We purchased it at the Lord's price. It needed many repairs, but the Lord had shown us what to do and supplied over the years for its completion.

It was now completed and we were content and enjoying the Lord's provision and He says, "It is time to move, son." Knowing the Lord always has a plan and a reason for what He does, I replied, "Yes Lord. But where do you want us to move to?"

"Trust the Lord. Lean not to your own understanding. Acknowledge Him in all your ways and He will direct the path." (Proverbs 3:5-6) The Lord had taught me to step out in a direction and He would order it (Isaiah 30:21).

Since the ministry had moved to the desert and we were looking to build a ministry center there, I started to look for a lot in the desert. (I had an impression that we were to build a house.) The night before I was to close the deal on the lot, the Lord gave me a dream.

In the dream, I saw myself praying on the hill where I had gone to pray for the past ten years. Upon awaking the next morning the desert lot was out of my heart. I knew the Lord wanted me to build the house on the hill where I prayed. But where on the hill?

The Lord had taught me just continue to trust and acknowledge Him. The Lord said, "Contact the realtor which I used to bless you on the other house. I want to bless him for blessing you." (The realtor had paid for our down payment so we could acquire our first home.)

Later, as I discovered, this man knew this area the best of anyone at that time. He showed us various lots. Each time we put in an offer. It did not work out. Rather than get discouraged, we continued to trust, thank, and acknowledge the Lord for His direction.

One day as I was praying I asked the Lord, "Father, I know that you have the lot here somewhere, but I do not know where it is!" He replied, "Drive up in." (I was in my car at the end of a dirt road.)

I drove up in the road a ways and got out of the car. There were peach orchards all around. The peace of God came upon me. I knew this was the lot. The Lord had directed the search.

I received a figure from the Lord to offer and contacted the broker the Lord wanted to bless with the sale and commission for having blessed Diana and I. The deal was made.

The Lord always leads in peace by the Holy Spirit. When you have the peace of God, then it is God's best. In a God deal every one comes out blessed — buyer and seller.

In the months following in God's wisdom we were being prepared for building the church by building this house. There is so much involved in building. One must continue to trust the Lord. "Lean not to your own understanding. Acknowledge Him in all your ways and He will direct the path." Praise the Lord.

I asked the Lord one day, "Why are we having all these difficulties?" He replied, "Because it is My will!"

Many people do not understand the Lord's will. They think it is God's will that they have problems, sickness, etc. It is not God's will that we have problems rather that we trust Him and He will see us through to His glory and will accomplished.

What the Lord was saying to me was that He wanted the house and the church built. The thief was attempting to hinder and steal what the Lord wanted to be done. The thief could not prevent what the Lord wanted because we trusted and obeyed the Lord and gave the Lord the praise for what was done was done to the glory of God in the will of God.

The Lord will make sure that His will will be done! Our part is to acknowledge and praise and thank Him and tell the people their faith in God is not in vain. Tell the people what great and wonderful things the Lord had done!

THE SPECIAL OFFERING

In the adventure of life with the Holy Spirit, everything happens for a purpose the Lord has ordained. If we lean to our own understanding we will be confused and upset. We must trust the Lord and learn to flow with what the Lord is doing. This is why wisdom (God's understanding) is the principle thing. Ask the Lord what He wants and what He is doing, and how He is doing it.

We had a special offering coming up in a few weeks. I had purposed to give a sizeable amount and had it ready for the offering.

One morning we woke up to discover our house furnace and water heater were not working. It was cold, and rain and snow were coming down.

Since we are tithers and offering (givers 10% of gross income first to the Lord) I prayed over the equipment that the thief could not steal from us in Jesus' name (Malachi 3:8-12). We have done this many times over the years and the Lord made things work or things did not breakdown or wear out.

No results appeared to happen. (We walk by faith and not by sight) continuing to thank and praise the Lord, the Lord spoke, "Let your fingers do the walking." (A reference to a yellow pages phone book commercial that I had heard.)

I pulled out the phone book to the "yellow pages" and looked at the plumbing-heating section. The commercial for a company from another city caught my eye as the Lord directed. I called them and amazingly they said they would be right out to help us.

The technician worked all day to service and replace the equipment. During this time as we were talking, he shared how his family had left him because of his personal problems. I proceeded to share the Lord with him. He received the Lord Jesus as his Lord and Savior, was filled with the Holy Spirit speaking in new tongues! He received prayer for his issues, asking the Lord's forgiveness and deliverance. We prayed that his family be healed and restored. I told him to go to a church which the Holy Spirit leads him to and to get water baptized.

He handed me the bill and I wrote him a check. As he walked down the driveway, I thought *"My special offering is gone!"*

Then the Lord spoke, "son, you just gave to Me — you sowed to Me. For what you do to the least of these you do to Me."

What the Lord was telling me was that if the furnace and water heater had not had the problems, I could never have met this man. He received the Lord and the blessing of heaven to his whole family through me. When I paid the bill, I gave my offering to the Lord (I was not stolen from! The Lord's purpose was accomplished!)

Two weeks later the Lord supplied me my special offering through an investment I had made. I was able to give ten thousand to the Lord, rather than one. The Lord increased and blessed my offering ten times. (2nd Corinthians 9)

I received a letter from the man stating that his entire family was back together going to church, and he had been water baptized. Praise the Lord!

LEAVE THE OIL ON

A man came to the ministry with his mother. His desire was to be free of homosexuality and to receive Jesus. As a result of his choice, all of his family and friends received the Lord Jesus, the Holy Spirit, and became part of the Lord's family — His Church. His sickness had left his body.

He was a bold witness for the Lord knowing that the Lord had given him a new life forever with Jesus who had become his first love. He gave up his old earthly lifestyle and lived in the Lord's heavenly lifestyle. (1st Corinthians 6)

Years later something attacked his body. I received a call from a family member that the doctors said that he would not live out the day.

Inquiring of the Lord, He said to me, "Go anoint him with oil." I went immediately. Finding the man in a semiconscious condition, I said, "It is Pastor. I am going to anoint you in the name of the Lord Jesus. The prayer of faith will heal you and raise you up. (James 5) In the name of Jesus — leave his body. Be healed in Jesus' name." I left the room.

From the report of the family, he lived out the day and night, not letting anyone touch or wipe off the oil. Whatever disease that had come on his body left him. He lived for several more years encouraging others in the faith and to live holy.

Several years later, he approached me and said, "Pastor, I believe the Lord Jesus is calling me to come and be with Him. I believe I have finished what the Lord has given me to do and I want to be with Jesus."

It was not long thereafter that he peacefully was received into Jesus' loving arms.

WHAT IS THE OUTCOME

After several lung procedures a woman lay in the hospital with no hope. Every time the medical people would say, "We will do this." Her hope would rise. Then it did not work. She would be discouraged. She grew despondent and depressed.

The Lord told me to go to the hospital and anoint her with oil in the name of Jesus, and to ask her a question. I went.

The question which I was to ask her has transformed many lives since that time. Jesus says, "Be it done to you according to your faith." What you are believing according to God's Word is what you will be receiving.

Hope is different than faith. (Hebrews 11:1) (See *Victory* book) She had given up her hope. I asked her the Lord's question. *"What do you see at the finish of what you are going through?"*

What you see happening at the end is what you are going to have for better or for worse. We cannot be looking at all the ups and downs of situation and circumstance. What matters is how this is going to end up or finish — the final results.

Explaining the James 5 anointing process caused her hope and faith to rise again. When I asked her, "What do you see at the finish?" She responded, "I see my lungs breathing perfectly well."

There was no more that could be done for her medically. She left the hospital that week breathing perfectly well for another eighteen years. She peacefully went to the Lord breathing perfectly well.

FISH IN A POND

Over the years we have seen the Lord heal and deliver people from about everything that could mentally or physically happen. The Lord is so good!

The Lord said to me, "Son, we are going to see even greater things." I replied, "How could we see greater things than you have already done?" He responded, "We are going to see more of what I do!"

The Lord's idea of "greater" is not necessarily more spectacular or extravagant. It is more correctly stated in increase or His function fulfilled. "He who would be great in the Kingdom of God must become the servant of all."

I was led of the Lord to attend a meeting at a church. As I sat there enjoying the Lord's Word, ministry, and the fellowship with other believers, I had a vision.

I saw fish in a pond. Suddenly one fish ate another fish. Then a larger fish ate that smaller fish. Then that fish was eaten by a larger fish and on and on. Then the Lord said, "Son, this should not be so in My church!"

Following the service, as the ministers made themselves available to the people, I stepped up recounting the vision to the minister. Tears came to the minister's eyes. Apparently, another larger ministry had just done this to them.

The Lord wants us encouraging each others life and ministry. Church growth should not happen at another ministry's expense. We are the Lord's Body and Team.

TEN HEALED

The Lord has used Joshua 1:5-9 to encourage me often over the years. One day when discouragement was attempting to set in using the thought, *"Where are all the people who have been healed and received life changing benefit?"*

The Holy Spirit reminded me that this happened to Jesus too. "Were there not ten healed and one has come back to give thanks to God."

"Give thanks to Me that all ten were healed and that one has come back to give thanks to Me!" the Lord said.

I am learning to thank the Lord for the ones who have received over the years and the ones He is sending — past, present, and future. Because I know that whoever believes upon the Lord Jesus Christ will not go away empty and will receive what the Lord has for them. What they do with it is between them and God.

My part is to do what the Lord gives me to do when He brings them to us — to love, enjoy, and care for them as long as they are with us. (Hebrews 13:7, 17)

TOUCH MY TONGUE

A doctor who worked with serious child issues referred a mother and her daughter to us knowing that the Lord worked through us on spiritual, mental, and physical issues. This child was four years old and had not spoken. At night she would make sounds like an animal. There was no peace in the home.

Upon touching her tongue and commanding the demonic influence off her in Jesus' name, the first word she spoke was "Jesus." I then let her wander around as the people loved her. The Holy Spirit wanted to minister to the mother.

When someone in the family is having trauma, everyone is having trauma. These people had been all over the country seeking help for their daughter. The mother began to cry. "I did not want to hope again." She stated.

So many times they had gotten their hope up only to be disappointed again. I noted the dad did not come. (Many people do not believe spiritual cures, or he had just given up hope.)

I explained that they must now continue in the Lord who makes them not ashamed because they put their trust in Him. We gave them faith and healing materials (Victory book, healing information, etc). We must continue in the Lord's Word and faith in Jesus.

Several weeks later the doctor told us that the family had said to be sure to tell us that the little girl was talking. She was not making the animal sounds and howling all night. Peace was in their home! Praise the Lord!

In another similar situation, another little girl was brought who did not talk. I touched her tongue in Jesus name, "Be loosed!" A very big voice came out of this very little girl. Later, her first word was "Jesus."

The mother told her friend to tell us that the child began talking "all the time." Praise the Lord!

In the early years of ministry a lady brought her 20 year old son to us. She was a nurse I later found out. As I began praying over him, the Lord revealed he had hearing problems.

My normal practice is to tell what is causing the hearing or (whatever) loss to leave and to speak healing in Jesus' name. For hearing conditions I go behind the person (I do not want them reading my lips) and ask them to repeat after me what I am saying.

When I started to do this, the young man kept trying to get me to stand in front of him. He wanted me to talk in front of him. I asked the Lord, "What is he doing?" The Lord replied, "He wants to see how you make the sounds he is now hearing."

I then realized this young man had been deaf and dumb. I moved in front of him so he could see how I moved my lips and tongue to make the sounds he was hearing.

Praise the Lord! His first words were "Thank you Jesus for healing me."

SERIOUS SERIES

While praying the Lord directed me to do a 13 week marriage and family series. He sent me to a city that was thirty minutes from where I lived.

I did the series each week. Upon completion I asked the Lord, "Why did you have us come to this city to do this teaching series?" (No one from that city came.) He replied, "I wanted hungry people."

Every one, including myself, that came drove a minimum of thirty minutes or in most cases more to attend weekly the seminar. The Lord wanted people who really were serious and wanted to learn and to change so they would draw out His best to make this marriage and family series. (See Marriage and Family materials.)

GARBAGE DETAIL

I tell people, "I am the garbage man, not the garbage can, so do not dump on me." The Lord assigned me to the detail that oftentimes helps people at the crisis, pain, traumatic, and worst moments of their lives. He then does amazingly impossible things for them bringing heaven and removing the work of darkness and destruction giving to them His faith, hope, and love.

One of the greatest joys I find in life is watching how the Holy Spirit can turn what the thief intends for evil to God's glory. We serve an awesome God. Each day I wake up I am so excited about what the Lord is going to do today and how He is going to do it!

I know whom I believe and I am fully persuaded that He is able to keep what I have committed to Him until it is completed or He returns. (2nd Timothy 1:12) It is such a privilege to come upside people in their worst moments knowing that the Lord is going to do something amazing for them to His glory and their good.

Thank you, Lord, for the privilege to serve you on your "garbage detail." Whatever the Lord has given to you to do, do it with all your heart in the name of Jesus to the glory of God. Your labor in the Lord is not in vain. You will see the glory of God. Do not give up or be overwhelmed by life and ministry. (Galatians 6:9)

The Lord told me, "Son, never lose the passion for the compassion! For I will never leave or forsake you. Destroy the works of the flesh, the world, and the devil. Bring heaven to My people for I am with you always. Bring them into My presence through My Word and My Spirit and they will know that I am who I am — the Almighty God. Nothing is too difficult for Me and I will do it for them!"

Ministers of God we need to be willing to step out and to allow God to change your life and ministry. Do not be afraid of the people and for your life or livelihood. Daily seek the Lord about what He wants you to do and how He wants you to do it.

Enjoy the life and ministry the Lord has given to you. Do it with all your heart to the Lord. Finish the work and receive the crowns the Lord has prepared for His faithful ones. I love you all and I know the Lord loves you more!

TALK WITH JESUS

Conversing with the Lord is one of my favorite things to do during the day and night. Above all I enjoy listening to Him.

Early in the ministry I thought it would be good if Jesus would just come and sit down and talk with me. (Similar to Peter wanting to set up camp [tents] and spend time with Jesus when the Jesus, Moses and Elijah were together.)

I had been seeking wisdom on some matters (James 1). As I was sitting in my chair, the Lord spoke. "Son, what are you doing?" I replied, "I thought it would be nice if you would come and sit down (appear) and talk with me." He said, "I am not going to do it. I have already shown you what you wanted to know."

Several weeks before the Lord had given me the understanding. I just thought it would be nice if He would appear and we could sit down and talk. He proceeded to tell me that I do not need to have Him appear to me because I know He is with me through His Word and promise. He affirmed His promises. (Hebrews 13:5-6, Matthew 18:20, Acts 10:38, Matthew 28:20)

The Lord only does what He takes pleasure in and only does what He wants to do. He told me, "Do likewise!" But He was not saying to seek the Lord, others, or myself to do what I take pleasure in or what I want to do.

The Lord was saying to me, "Son, you do what I take pleasure in and what I want you to do (the Lord's will and purpose).

GIFT OF FAITH

Faith comes by hearing the Word and promise of God. There exists another kind of faith which supernaturally comes by the Holy Spirit to enable power to produce a miracle to occur over a period of time (1st Corinthians 12:9). It is used to impart the Holy Spirit, to cast out devils, raise the dead, pronounce blessing, work miracles and healings. There is no possibility of doubt when this God faith is operating.

Unlike the other two supernatural power gifts of the Holy Spirit (gifts [plural] of healing and working of miracles) (1st Corinthians 12:9-10) which manifest instantly, the gift of faith works in time.

Because of what the Lord has called us to do we often see these power gifts of the Holy Spirit operating as the Holy Spirit wills and directs. The Lord accomplishes His purpose however He wants to do it through whatever means He desires to use. We just believe Him and act on His Word in Jesus' name! The Lord makes the people whole to His glory!

For instance we have seen the Lord heal many cases of head trauma over the years. On several occasions the people had fallen off the roof on their heads. The Lord saved their lives. No brain or physical damage occurred in their body as the Lord healed over time.

Many people who were in car and motorcycle crashes were restored to life fully functioning mentally and physically over time. Many in a coma for a week to three months. They were diagnosed in many cases if they lived to be "no more than a vegetable." They are living and functioning today because of the gift of faith and the Lord's goodness.

The Lord says, "My people perish for lack of knowledge" and many do not want God's knowledge. (Hosea 4:6) People need to be taught the "God kind of faith" (Mark 11:22-25). I have seen people who were operating in the "God kind of faith" receive the "God kind of results."

Someone came to me one time saying, "I did everything you said but it did not work." I told them, "You did not do what I said (in reality what the Lord said) because it is impossible for the Lord to not do what He says He will do (Numbers 23:19) <u>if you act on His Word</u>. If you are double-minded and doubt you cannot expect to receive anything from God (James 1:6-8).

People say, "Why are some healed and others not?" I respond, "why are some saved and others not? They do not believe! The Lord wants everyone saved, delivered, and healed from the devil's rule. Jesus says, "The thief comes to steal, kill, and destroy. But I have come that you might have life and more abundantly." (John 10:10)

There are many factors involved in why people do not receive from God: double minded, ignorance, pride, unbelief. Personally, I spent 22 years of my life in and out of hospitals. Since I learned and believed, the Lord's principles I have not been sick, but five days in 42 years since then. I caused the 5 days by overworking.

I love the honesty of the man in Mark 9:17. He wants his boy healed. He says to Jesus, "If you can do anything take pity on us." Jesus replies, "If you can. Everything is possible for him who believes." The man responds, "I do believe; help me overcome my unbelief." He received from heaven for his son to God's glory and to their good.

It is not about pity about the situation. It is all about faith in God. In countless encounters we have seen the devil's work destroyed by the faith in the name of Jesus. (Acts 10:38) God's faith works by His love and destroys the work of the devil accomplishing God's good to His glory.

One lady we prayed for always got well when we prayed. But then she would be sick again. The Lord told me, "She does not want to be well." (When she was "sick" then her husband had to stay home and take care of her. Some like attention.) I learned not everyone wants to be well. Some who were healed still wanted to be receiving disability checks, etc.

To get the Lord's results we have to learn from the Lord what the person is believing. Ask them. In one situation we were called into the baby newborn child of a couple was dying in the hospital.

As I spoke with them, it was evident that they were not saved. I explained salvation and healing to them. We prayed and they received Jesus as their Lord and Savior seeking God's forgiveness. We believed for the baby as well. The child is covered by the faith of the believing parents (1st Corinthians 7:14).

Over the next weeks, we saw the child moved from intensive care, recovering and returned to a normal room. One day I felt like something had pierced my heart. I rushed to the hospital to find the child back on "life support." I inquired of the Lord what was going on and I submitted the child to the Lord's loving care and went to the parent's home.

They greeted me. I asked them why they dropped their faith. They said to me, "We felt the child would be better off with Jesus." It was done according to their faith. The child died, when I believe and saw every evidence that the child would live.

It is true that we are better off with Jesus. Thought we die, yet shall we live (John 11). It takes no faith to die or see none of heavens promises. It does take faith in Jesus as Lord if you are going to have salvation when you die.

If it were better to die and be with Jesus, than I guess it would be better to believe that you would die when you are sick. People do not have to be in poverty, lonely, or broke and may need to die or get raptured so you will not be persecuted for your faith.

Jesus says, I came to enable you to have abundant life. Right now as well as forever. This takes faith in God and His promises. The Lord wants us to finish what He has given us to do. Bring heaven to people before we go to Jesus.

Paul says for me to live is Christ and to die is gain, but I must stay and help others until I have finished what the Lord gave me to do. (Philippians 2:26) I agree and that is the only reason I am still here is to proclaim, encourage, and help people to receive and stay in the love of God, to believe and act on God's Word to see the Lord's life.

I hate evil, pride, selfishness, unbelief, ignorance, strife, unforgiveness, poverty, lies, sickness and disease, fear and all the results that come from these things. The Lord hates these things because they cause people to not have heaven's best.

One evening a horrible car crash occurred. Four girls in the car. Two died instantly. Two sent to the hospital. Both forecasted to die.

The normal response of people when tragedy occurs is a flurry of fear, grief and prayers hoping that the Lord does something. Everyone calls, comes to the hospital sits there trying to comfort each other's grief hoping that the Lord does something. "My people perish for lack of knowledge." Hope is not faith.

As the days go by the prognosis of the circumstance and situation grows worse, the crowd dwindles and decreases until a few remain. I have seen it many times. People are dealing with their own grief, fears, issues, and faith or lack of it. The patient remains on their bed.

A verse that has bothered me since I was a little boy is Jesus saying, "Will there be faith found on the earth when I return." (Luke 18:18) With intensity I say, "yes, Lord, there will be 'the God-like kind of faith" when you return!"

Both girls were in a coma for days. The mother of one of the girls had been with the ministry for many years. She had become a woman of God and filled with the Holy Spirit and delivered of many things. She had learned and knew the Word of God.

Believing the Lord for her daughter and the other girl, she attempted to encourage the other family to continue to believe and not give up, but they had not been taught the Word of faith. As the days went by and the reports grew worse, they did not want to hear about holding on to hope and faith. They were preparing themselves for their daughter to die.

Disturbed and frustrated that she could not get them to believe, I encouraged her to love them and just be there for them. (We do not judge people, but seek to come up side them where they are. If they want more, so be it.)

The week before the Lord had told her through us, "Fear not! Only believe and she will wake up from the coma perfectly well!"

I walked into her room the day she woke up from the coma perfectly well. (It was like she was sleeping and just woke up.) The other girl had died.

"Pastor, she exclaimed with joy. Give me a hug!" I was overjoyed in what the Lord had done for her — just like He had said. She now has a husband and child and is doing well.

GIVE A MILLION

All of my life I have wanted to give a million dollars at one time to the Lord and His ministry. I have worked and tithed giving offerings to the Lord since I was a young boy. In preparation for the building cutting my salary in half for six years gave a significant sum to the ministry, but I still had not come near my goal that was in my heart to do.

Following a wonderful revival in which the Lord had done powerful things, I was driving home. The Lord brought to my remembrance my desire (which I know He had put in my heart). (Psalm 37)

I had been a little discouraged because I wanted so bad to do this. The Lord encouraged me. He said, "Son, you have already given to Me a million dollars at one time. In fact, it has been multiple millions. I led you by My Spirit to make investments which made millions for My Kingdom and ministry. You did not keep any for yourself, but rather gave it to Me. If you were of the world, you would have kept it for yourself, but you never thought it was yours because what you did, you did for Me. You have given your desire and more — you have given yourself to Me as I have given Myself to you."

"Delight in the Lord and He will give and fulfill His desires in you." (Psalm 37)

CRUNCHING GLASSES

As I moved down the prayer line a man stood in front of me took off his glasses and crunched them with his hand. "Why did you do that?" I asked. "As an act of my faith." He replied.

Sometimes people try to prove that they have faith by doing certain actions. It is like they are attempting to force something to happen.

I told the man that he would not need those glasses because the Lord had touched his eyes, but that he would wear several other pairs of glasses before his eyes would be restored to 20/20.

It happened the way the Lord had shown.

TO FORGIVE OR NOT

A lady with a white cane was ushered into service. She had come in support of her friend who had been in a serious car accident. Her friend had come for prayer a few weeks earlier. Her back was completely restored and she no longer needed the braces and the pain medication. (We often see the Lord heal bone and trauma issues.)

The blind lady came forward with her friend to the prayer line. Giving thanks to the Lord her friend testified about what the Lord had done for her and described her healing of her back.

When I came to the blind lady, I said to her, "You have someone in your life you need to forgive." She fell to the ground. The power of God had come upon her. I continued to pray for others.

Coming back to the blind lady who was now standing in the line, I asked her, “What happened?” She replied, “Something evil left my body!” I asked, “What caused you to go blind?”

She recounted her story. There is always a story or a moment at which things begin. Her story was that four years prior she had become involved in a terrible law suit with her best friend. Anger, bitterness, unforgiveness filled her heart. One morning she woke up completely blind. Both optic nerves were diagnosed as dead. She would never see again!

When the Lord diagnosed her problem, I did not pray for her sight to be restored. The Lord said, “You have someone in your life you need to forgive.” As she lay on the floor she forgave her “best” friend and “something evil left her body” by her admission.

You cannot remain in a state of anger, bitterness and unforgiveness, fear, and worry, etc. and expect anything good to come to you. To the contrary you give the devil the opportunity to steal, kill, and destroy. (Ephesians 4:26, Mark 11:26)

This is what had happened to this precious woman and to countless others over the years. The Lord sent forth His Word (the word of knowledge) revealing past or present things in people’s lives so they could be set free. He or she whom the Lord has set free is free indeed (John 8:36).

The blindness was the result of her unforgiveness! People just do not seem to understand that evil produces evil results. Spiritually, mentally, physically, financially, and in relationships. Unforgiveness is evil. Fear is evil. Unbelief is evil. Worry and selfishness is evil.

Jesus says, “Which is it easier to say — your sins be forgiven or take up your bed and walk?” Submit yourself to God (ask forgiveness) then resist the devil and he will flee from you (James 4:7).

I tell people if there is one person that you do not forgive, you are in danger of going to hell. Jesus cannot forgive you because you do not forgive others. (Matthew 18, Mark 11:26) Father, forgive us our trespasses *as we forgive* others. (Luke 6:37)

The work of darkness must be exposed so heaven might come to the person. That day heaven came to the blind lady. As we were talking, a discovery process began. She exclaimed with joy, "How light this room is!"

The Lord had restored her sight. (I did not know that completely blind people do not see light and darkness. They only see grey.) Then she started seeing and describing objects, colors, patterns. (It was so much fun enjoying her discovering the awesomeness of sight that most people take for granted.) There was not a dry eye in the place when she discovered and hugged her friend she had come with describing the clothes and colors she was wearing. Awesome God!

Optic nerves do not regenerate. I do not know what the Lord did so she could see, but she was seeing perfectly and describing everything she saw from the eyes of someone who was born again forgiven and clean fresh and new. (See Blind Lady Tape)

We have seen many creative miracles over the years where the Lord enables the person to have babies, see, hear, walk (no knee caps) where their parts are not there or are dead, etc.

This was not about this woman being healed of blindness. It was about the Lord's divine appointment loving her, showing her her sin, forgiving her (1st John 1:9) and then destroying the work of the devil. (Unforgiveness and resulting in physical blindness.) The Lord saved, healed, and delivered her giving her heaven and a whole new life abundantly now and forever.

Oh, I cannot forget she was also filled with the Holy Spirit speaking in tongues giving thanks to God well.

If you have someone you have not forgiven, in the name of Jesus, I encourage you to forgive them and reconcile right now so you can be forgiven! Remember this account and what Jesus said to a man that was healed, "go and sin no more, least a worse thing come upon you." (John 5:14)

People say, "I love and forgive everyone else except that person (put their name in). How would it be on the last day and Jesus looks at you and says, "I loved and forgave everyone else, but you! Go to darkness away from Me."

Unforgiveness and sin are not an option for a Christian!

TELL THE TRUTH

Diana and I sought to teach the children to always tell the truth. We would tell the truth to each other. The Spirit of the Lord is the Spirit of Truth. God hates liars because it is not love. The devil is the father of all liars. All liars will go to hell (Revelations 21:8). Integrity and respect are the keys to all relationships.

One day my neighbor was knocking on my front door. As I greeted him, he said, "Your children have ruined everything!" He was very angry and upset.

This man's wife had ran off with another man and left him and his five year old son alone together. He was living with his parents and was doing his best to relate to and care for his son.

"Everything I have worked so hard to do for my son your children have wrecked!" He had been teaching his son that Santa Clause was real, and making his home like a Santa's village and he dressed up as Santa.

Apparently my children had boldly told his son that Santa was not real. Christmas is about Jesus and that he had not been told the truth.

"What are you going to do about this with your children," he shouted at me. I thought he wanted to fight.

"Settle down," I softly said. (A soft answer turns away wrath.) "I know you are trying to do something good for your son because you love him. But the day is going to come when your son is going to find out the truth that there is no Santa. Then he is going to think that you lied to him, and he will not trust what you tell him. Would it not be better to tell him the truth about Santa and Jesus?"

He became quiet and replied, "Yes, I guess it would." "Here, I have some Bible story books about Jesus that you can read to him if you like."

He received the materials and thanked me. Later, I spoke to my children about the importance of speaking the truth in love. I commended them for speaking the truth, and they needed to understand the reasoning as to why people lie.

The wounds of a friend (for telling the truth to you) are faithful, trustworthy, and true. The truth may hurt but it will produce the Lord's results and purpose.

I know and wanted my children and the people of God to know the Lord's truth. I am responsible and accountable to the Lord, myself, and God's people for every word and deed that I do and say. Someday I will give an account to the Lord!

THE LORD'S HUMOR

As with Jesus, we have seen the Lord do many things in different ways to His glory and the good of His people.

One day we were enjoying the Word of God with a few people and the Lord spoke on "What mountain?" He was referring to the verse in Mark 11:22-25. We are speaking to the mountain to move in Jesus' name. The Lord was saying, "No problem. I do not see an issue!"

A lady came into the prayer line. She had a sixteen pound tumor in her womb. With the God-like kind of faith we spoke to the tumor "Be isolated (contained) and dry up from the roots, in Jesus' name!"

Several weeks later, she had surgery. The physicians discovered the tumor to have shrunken to the size of a small dried up plum and it was in a clear plastic like substance. They snipped it, took it out, and threw it away.

The Lord not only shrank and shriveled the sixteen pound tumor to nothing. He bagged it, so the physicians could clip it out and throw it in the trash. Praise be the Lord! God teamwork and humor.

The Lord laughs from the heavens at whatever opposes Him. His will, and His purpose from being accomplished (Psalm 2).

INTERCESSION

Upon arriving home, I discovered Diana upon the bed. She was having labor pains. The problem was that she was not pregnant.

As we were praying together in the Holy Spirit (tongues), she got up and went to the bathroom. As she looked into the toilet she saw blood and placenta. Instantly it was gone!

She reported this to me and I asked the Lord what was happening. I saw the face of a young lady who had not been able to carry a child and had several miscarriages. She was four months pregnant at that moment.

I called her to see what was transpiring with her. She said, "I was cramping and felt I was losing the baby. Suddenly the cramps all went away!"

The Lord had saved the baby. Diana, in God's compassion, had taken her place in intercession. Diana went through the pain, cramps, birthing and aborting process. The mother kept the child in her womb. Full term months later, the mother delivered a beautiful baby girl, and was able to have several other children.

The Lord be praised! Jesus is our intercessor!

THE TEST

Following a long four year design and building permit process, the ministry was ready to build the facility the Lord had planned. This had been a part of a thirty year vision given in 1984

One night as I was sleeping, the Lord gave me a dream in which I saw a pastor friend of mine in a deep depression, sitting holding his head and intensely weeping. It was a two part dream.

The Lord told me to go to him, love and help, and encourage him by sharing the dream. I called him and we met at a coffee shop he had chosen. As I shared with him what the Lord had shown me, tears filled his eyes. He knew the Lord had heard his prayer and loved him.

He had worked for several years attempting to build his church building and nothing worked out. He was tired and discouraged ready to give up the ministry.

As he listened and we prayed, he became more and more encouraged. The Lord lifted the depression and hope and joy came back to him. He knew the Lord loved him and his labor in the Lord was not in vain.

Part two of the dream involved me first talking with our boards. I explained to them what the Lord had instructed us to do. We prayed and they unanimously agreed.

The following day I drove to the pastor's office. He was excited to see me and we shared vision. When it was my turn to share, I recounted with him the second part of the dream — the Lord's instruction.

"The Lord told me and our boards are in agreement that we are to give to you and your ministry our project" — approved plans, land, etc. He sat stunned.

"You have spent years, put millions of dollars, and your life into this project. How can you now, just give it away to us?" He exclaimed.

I replied, "It is not ours! It is all the Lord's project. We are all the Lord's. He directs what He wants, how He wants it, and when He wants it to be done. We just love, honor, and obey what He directs us to do!"

"I cannot believe this! You are a better man than I am. This is too wonderful! I will have to talk to my board." He was trying to figure this all out.

He continued, "What will you do if we do not accept this very generous gift?" He could not believe that this was happening to him. Then he thought (trying to figure out our motivation thinking we possibly could not finish the project so we were giving it to them. Or he did not want us to give away something we had worked so hard, long, and at such great price on. (He realized all that he had sacrificed to do what they had worked on with no success and now it was given to them with no effort on their part. It was too awesome to comprehend.)" They had the money to build this.

I replied, "If you do not want to receive and proceed on the project, I guess we will just have to proceed and build the project. Take a few weeks, talk to your board, and let me know whether or not you decide to receive the gift and proceed or not."

A few weeks later I received a call thanking the Lord and us for the offer, but they declined. "Pastor Randy, I believe the Lord is testing you, like Abraham was tested by God about sacrificing (or giving up) his son of promise Isaac. Because you were willing and obedient to do the Lord's direction, the Lord will always continue to bless your efforts and life. You did not seek anything for yourself or consider it yours, but rather chose to honor the Lord and give glory to Him."

The Lord spoke a word of wisdom and blessing to us that day. We had passed the Lord's test. Everything is the Lord's and for His glory. Later after the Lord completed the building, the words the Lord had spoken to me were very clear in my heart and mind, "I will fill this house with My Glory!"

NO OTHER GODS

As the helicopter flew closer, we could see clearly the 700 year old temple which the lava from the volcano had not touched as it went around the temple. The helicopter pilot who was guiding us believed in this god as he preached faith in his god to us. "My god caused the lava to go right around her temple."

It was evident that the lava had gone right around the temple. That night on our way back to our residence, the rain began to fall, lightly at first and then torrential so great that I could no longer see the road. Rivers of water were flowing all around us. In the darkness we were lost.

"Lord Jesus help us get to safety. Cover us with the blood of Jesus. Protect us from evil, Lord. We bind these forces of darkness in Jesus' name!" I was praying as Diana and the children were praying in the

Holy Spirit speaking in the tongues. Something was trying to kill us.

Suddenly out of nowhere I saw a pair of rear lights in front of us. I followed the lights of the car as it navigated a road that was no longer there as it had turned into a river of water. Then the car began to wind its way up a hillside which took us to high ground and safety. If the Lord had not guided our path, we may have taken the low road which could have caused great harm.

That night I had a serious dark dream. Demonic activity was all around. I woke up in a sweat. The Lord spoke, "Son, there is not a move of My Spirit in this place. Pray for a move of My Spirit and put the blood of Jesus over the temple." I did so.

We returned home. A few months later an article appeared in the newspaper — "Nothing seems to stop Hawaii volcano eruption."

The volcano erupted again and this time buried the temple under the lava. The Lord will not have other gods before Him. The Lord began a move of His Spirit on the island.

TO BE OR NOT BE GREAT

Jesus' disciples were always positioning and desiring greatness for themselves. Jesus presented a servant model for greatness in the kingdom. He washed their feet. Jesus did not seek recognition or promotion for Himself, but rather desired glory for His heavenly Father living and working towards that goal.

Pressure comes on the minister of God to have a "large" congregation or "worldwide" influence. We cannot get into striving, comparing, and competition with one another. We must be faithful to do what the Lord has given to each of us to do, no more or no less! Jesus said, "All the Father has for me will come to me." (John 6:37)

The Lord does not judge a minister on the size of the ministry outreach. To the contrary, the Lord judges the ministers by their faithfulness to the calling the Lord has assigned to each one. No one can take to himself something that the Lord has not given from heaven. (John 3:27)

One time when the Lord Jesus was teaching me about this He said, "I would have been considered a failure by many ministers today. Everyone left and rejected me. Yet I fulfilled what I was given to do by My Father and He exalted Me above every name. (Philippians 2)

Jeremiah would have been considered a failure, yet he said and did everything I gave him to do. No one received his message which I had given him, but he remained faithful to Me!

It will be the same with you. Those who have ears to hear will hear. Those who do not, will not hear what My Spirit says to them through you. Some will receive others will not because they do not believe Me. They will not believe you. Do not be discouraged or afraid of them. Say what I give you to say and do what I give you to do to those that I will send to you. We will reach the world one person at a time.

A church of 10 or 30 thousand is not much in an area of 5 to 10 million people. Much work is still needed to be done. Be not impressed by numbers, but rather impressed by My Spirit and My Presence (glory) which I will display when you honor and obey Me," saith the Lord.

Friends, you never know what the Lord is going to do with what you are faithful to be, say and do by His Spirit's direction. The Lord said to me, "Son, you will never know all the lives that I am touching and changing through you to My glory." Your labor in the Lord is not in vain.

We have seen where the Lord has used the materials He has given to us. They were believed, shared and used by others. The Lord touched more people's lives through them ministering and sharing the materials than we ever would have reached in many nations of the world. "Lord, bless your ministry through Your ministers!"

In one example, the Lord discipled a young man off the streets in Canada through some people we minister with using the Lord's materials He had given and supplied through us. This young man grew in the Lord and is ministering to millions of people worldwide. He is fulfilling what the Lord gave him to do. May he be faithful to the end.

John the Baptist said, "He must increase and I must decrease." He was speaking about how he was completing his role in God's team and Jesus was coming in to His role.

Another minister in Africa played one of the messages the Lord gave us. His life and many others changed. He went on to change many other's lives through the Holy Spirit.

Enjoy the Lord's life and ministry in and through you and others. We are family and team.

THE LORD'S ENCOURAGEMENT

The devil seeks to undermine the minister's confidence and ministry through many ways using our strengths and weaknesses against us. We must be alert to his wily schemes. There is nothing hidden that will not be revealed. The Lord will expose the work of darkness.

If the devil could not distract me from loving the Lord, he went after separating me from the people. Because I love the people so much, the thief came to me through some people who had plans to take over the ministry (Lucifer spirit).

Like Korah came to Moses saying, "You take to yourself too much!" (Numbers 16), these people came to me saying, "The people love you too much!" They knew my desire was for the people to love the Lord, not to lift me up.

Their goal was for me to withdraw from the people, so they could step in and take over the ministry by me delegating more and more things to them. They wanted the people to go to them, rather than to me. (Absolom did this sitting at the gate telling the people, "My dad is busy, but I can help you."

The Lord had me go to a minister's conference. As I was enjoying the fellowship and ministry, the Lord spoke, "Son, the people cannot love you enough! You are the one I use to bring them My Word and My Ministry. You are the one I use to love and care for them. They cannot love you enough! I love you through them as I love them through you! I have made you, the people, and I ONE together to and for My glory. Be encouraged!"

Seeing the lie of the devil through these people, I went home in the power of the Holy Spirit with bold confidence that I was right where the Lord wanted me to be — in the Love of my Father loving His people with the love of the Lord and they loving me with the love of my Father.

As I drew near to the Lord and the people, these people who were being used by the devil were dealt with by the Lord as I loved them even more. The devil's scheme was destroyed. The Lord was glorified. All the people were loved and blest. I was strengthened, refreshed, and encouraged by the Lord.

AN HONORABLE CALLING

Being a minister of the Lord is not a job or a common activity. It is an honorable calling. That is why I prefer the title… reverend… over my professional doctorate titles. We represent the Lord Jesus in this world. It is a holy calling from the Lord, not man.

The apostle Paul says, "unlike so many, we do not peddle the word of God for profit. On the contrary, in Christ we speak before God with sincerity, like men sent from God… (2 Cor. 2:17) (see 2 Cor.10-11).

Personally, I do not care about what office or title I have. I am a servant of God. People ask, "Are you an apostle, prophet, evangelist, pastor or teacher?" My reply is, " let the fruit and the work speak for itself. The Lord be honored and praised! I am just a servant on a team doing what the Lord has given me to do by His grace." (1 Cor.3-4)

FINISH STRONG

Our lives are a moment in eternity. Jesus finished His assignment. In John 21:25, it says that Jesus did many other things well. If every one of them were written down, even the whole world would not have room for the books that would be written.

Jesus in us is the hope of glory. The acts of the Holy Spirit continue today through the Lord's servants of whom I am one of many.

We are dedicated to the Lord Jesus Christ with every fiber of our being. We are children of Heaven, joint heirs with our Lord to all that He is, has, and does, in Heaven (2nd Peter 1:3-7) and in the earth. We are born again for such a time as this!

The apostle Paul says, "It is time for my departure. I have fought the good fight. I have finished the course. I have kept the faith. Now there is in store for me the crown of righteousness, which the Lord, the righteous judge, will award to me on that day — and not only to me, but also to all who have longed for His appearing." (2nd Timothy 4:7-8)

We must remain faithful to the end and receive the crown of life which the Lord has promised to those who love Him. (James 1:12) Finish what you have been given. Finish Strong!

Now may the God of peace who brought up our Lord Jesus from the dead, that great Shepherd of the sheep, through the blood of the everlasting covenant, make you complete in every good work to do His will, working in you what is well pleasing in His sight, through Jesus Christ to whom be glory forever and ever. Amen. (Hebrews 13:20-21)

FOR A COMPLETE LIST OF BOOKS AND MINISTRY RESOURCES BY THE AUTHOR, CONTACT:

Randy C. Brodhagen
Glory to God Ministries International
67-399 Palm Canyon Drive, Cathedral City, CA, 92234
Mailing Address: P.O. Box 4167, Palm Springs, CA 92263
United States of America

Phone: 760-321-5222
Email: pastor@glorytogod.org
Internet: www.glorytogod.org